# STEELHEAD COUNTRY

With every good wish,

Steve Raymond

## BOOKS BY STEVE RAYMOND

*Kamloops*

*Backcasts*

*The Year of the Angler*

*The Year of the Trout*

*Steelhead Country*

# STEELHEAD
# COUNTRY

Angling
in
Northwest
Waters

Steve Raymond
Illustrations by Gordon Allen

SASQUATCH BOOKS
SEATTLE

Printed in the United States of America.

Published and distributed by Sasquatch Books.
Distributed in Canada by Raincoast Books, Ltd.

Originally published as a hardcover edition in 1991 by Lyons & Burford, Publishers, New York, NY.

Library of Congress Cataloging in Publication Data
    Raymond, Steve.
        Steelhead country : angling in Northwest waters /
    Steve Raymond; illustrations by Gordon Allen.
            p. cm.
    Originally published: New York : Lyons & Burford, 1991.
        ISBN 1-57061-014-2  $9.95
            1. Steelhead fishing—Northwest, Pacific. 2. Fly
        fishing—Northwest, Pacific. I. Title.
        [SH687.7.R39        1991]
        799.1'755—dc20                                91-12073
                                                         CIP


Sasquatch Books
1008 Western Avenue
Seattle, Washington 98104
(206) 467-4300

Sasquatch Books publishes high-quality nonfiction and children's titles related to the Northwest. For more information about our books, contact us at the above address and number.

# FOR

*Enos Bradner and Ralph Wahl*

# CONTENTS

# PROLOGUE

T HE NORTHWESTERN tip of North America leans over the Pacific Ocean like an old cedar limb weighted down with rain. The limb has a long reach and casts a long shadow that falls all the way down to the northern California coast. Out of that shadow ten thousand rivers run.

In these rivers the steelhead trout evolved.

Probably the steelhead could have come from nowhere else but this misty, dark corner of the world. It is a realm of vast landscapes, of cold mountain rivers flowing down through silent, shadowed forests, of relentless gray skies and unremitting rain, of ragged coastlines honeycombed with hidden harbors and secret bays where bright rivers mingle with the sea.

Certainly the steelhead is well matched to this environment in all respects—in its color, in its shape and strength, even in its temperament. It can be as dour as the misty weather one day and as bold as bright sunshine on the next. It fits into the rivers smoothly and easily, blending with the camouflage of their rubbled bottoms or disappearing into the deep shade from fir and cedar limbs along their banks. It is elusive and mysterious, but also strong and spirited enough to force its way upstream against the momentum and force of the vast weight of water ever spilling down from the foothills and the snowy peaks beyond them.

The steelhead is born in the quick and lively waters of these mountain rivers and it spends its early life feeding and growing in their shallow shaded runs until it feels the first tugs of the migratory instinct coded deeply in its genes. Then it rides the spring torrents down to the ocean and makes its way along fog-shrouded passages winding through a labyrinth of offshore islands until at last it finds itself alone beneath the broad Pacific swells. Following strong currents that flow like invisible rivers through the sea, it sets forth on a great feeding migration far to the north and west where it mingles in the trackless ocean with thousands of others of its kind, born of hundreds of other rivers.

For months or even years the steelhead continues on this journey, growing ever larger and stronger as it forages in the rich dark pastures of the ocean until finally, deep inside, it feels the seeds of its offspring take root and begin to grow. And then, in response to some exquisite mechanism of natural timing, it obeys an instinctive urge to turn toward home.

Back it comes, swimming now against the invisible currents that have borne it so far, pressing onward until the clouded coast is once again within its reach. As it enters the sheltered coastal waters it somehow perceives the scent of its home river, unique from all others, and follows that scent back to the estuary it left so many months before. There it waits restlessly for a rising tide to boost it back into the familiar current where it first knew life.

Only a few come back of all the silvery host that left the river years before, only the few that were quick and strong enough to survive all the predators and perils of the long journey. But those few have grown into mighty fish, fat and strong with the stored-up energy of the ocean, streamlined in shape to breast the forceful current, bright as the gleam of sunlight reflected from a wave.

Little wonder it is, then, that anglers wait anxiously for the steelhead's return. This they have always done, from the days when Indians fished only for food and sport was an unknown concept, and this they still do in greater numbers than ever be-

fore. Now the riverbanks are lined with long ranks of weekend anglers, a fresh gantlet of rods waits at every turn of the river, and each returning steelhead faces a new test at every foot of its upstream journey.

The fishermen wait and scheme and fuss with a great singleness of purpose for a chance to grapple with one of the few returning fish. They know, either from hearsay or experience, that hooking a steelhead is a little like hooking a lightning bolt, that the fight of their lives awaits them, and they look forward to it with a degree of anticipation and perseverance that is impossible for a nonfisherman to understand.

But for the steelhead there is a heartbreaking finality to these struggles for life, so close to completion of its long journey—unless, as now happens more and more frequently, the victorious angler is willing to settle for the memory rather than the fish itself, and the exhausted steelhead is returned to the river to rest, recover, and continue on its way.

The return of the steelhead is an integral part of life in the great Pacific Northwest. A whole tradition has grown up around it, a tradition with a complicated code of behavior and ethics, a complex set of tactics, and a growing body of literature and lore to which each succeeding generation of anglers contributes its own share. The steelhead has become a fish of legend in tales told around the campfires that flicker on countless riverbanks in the raining dawn, or in tall stories swapped over steaming cups of coffee in the greasy-spoon diners of little towns clustered along the rivers. There are other great fishing traditions, but none quite the same as this. Perhaps one must be born in the Pacific Northwest, or at least spend much of his life here, to fully understand and become a part of it.

The initiation rite is to spend hundreds of long days under leaden skies oozing endless rain, to feel the sudden crackle of energy that comes on those wonderful rare mornings when the sun rises in a cloudless sky and reveals the country in all its freshly washed splendor, to stand for countless cold hours in icy gray rivers while the hope for a steelhead burns lower and lower, to struggle to tie a leader knot with cracked and frozen fingers while cold rain trickles down your neck. It is to search miles of shrunken summer river under a boiling sun in a vain quest for a steelhead, to wade and cast and wade and cast for hours or even days on end without so much as the sign of even a single fish—and then to experience the explosive, helpless, breath-robbing excitement that comes in the split second when a steelhead finally does take with a strike that shakes your arms all the way to their sockets, to see the unforgettable sight of the fish's first cartwheeling leap, its sides flashing with a brighter light than day.

All these things, and more, are part of the steelhead tradition. Long may it continue.

# STEELHEAD
# COUNTRY

# 1 | NATURAL SELECTION

THE PROCESS of natural selection is a ruthless means of refinement, a sort of evolutionary editing process that separates the wheat from the chaff, the strong from the weak, the specific from the random, and assures that only the best and the fittest species will survive. That it applies to fish, including the steelhead trout, is almost universally known; that it also applies to fishermen is not so well known.

Its application to steelhead begins the very moment an adult lays her eggs in the cold gravel of the river. Of all the thousands of eggs that spill from her vent, only a fraction will escape hungry predators, deadly fungus and suffocating silt to survive to hatching. Of those that hatch, grow into alevins and struggle up from the gravel into the open river, only a few will elude the even more efficient predators that await them there—swift kingfishers, patient herons, hungry Dolly Varden.

Of those that escape predators, only a few will survive the fierce competition for food with others of their own kind, or avoid being trapped in drying potholes when the river shrinks to its summer flow. And of the pitiful few that pass all these tests and trials, only a tiny fraction will live the year or two it takes a young steelhead to grow to smolting size.

Even then the process does not end. When the young smolts travel down to the sea, they are quickly exposed to a host of hungry new predators—seals, killer whales, sea lions, cormorants, and any number of other threats that will stalk them relentlessly on their long feeding journey across the North Pacific and all the way back again. Few survive this long passage, and for each hundred hatchlings only one or two, if any at all, will return safely as adult fish to the rivers of their birth.

The process of natural selection among fishermen is fortunately not so ruthless or so final, but it is by no means less efficient: For every small boy who first goes forth to fish with drugstore rod and can of worms, only a few will resist all the distractions of modern life and keep their love of angling with them as they grow to adults. Of these, only a fraction will prove themselves immune to the lure of other species such as trout, salmon, bass, or panfish, and learn to fish for steelhead. And of these, only a small percentage will ever grow in skill beyond the ranks of casual weekend or opening-day anglers.

Nor does the process end there. Even among dedicated steelhead fishermen, only a few will graduate beyond the use of bait or lure and take up the ultimate challenge of steelhead fly fishing. For each hundred boyhood anglers, perhaps only one or two, if any at all, will learn the patience and skill it takes to capture steelhead on the fly. But theirs will be among the greatest rewards in angling.

I know this because I am a survivor of the process. It did not come as easily or as quickly for me as it sometimes does for others, but I am grateful that at last it did come—for now I can count myself among the fortunate few who have witnessed the rare and graceful rise of a great steelhead to a floating fly, who

have felt the power of mighty rivers and the breathless excitement of a wild fish on a long run that threatens the limits of the tackle and the skill of the angler. These are things that defy description—they must be felt—and many are the anglers who will never feel them.

All my life I have fished. I was born in the Pacific Northwest, in the very heart of trout and steelhead country, and some of my earliest memories are of the moist smell of riverbanks or the musty scent of weed-filled trout ponds. In my mind's eye I can still see the well-worn path along the creek that flowed within a mile of my boyhood home, see myself kneeling there with a short telescoping steel rod, awkwardly lowering a lump of bait down into the mysterious amber-colored water with wild hopes that an unwary trout would dart from cover and impale itself on the tiny hidden hook. It happened just often enough to keep me interested, and as a result the knees of my jeans were always worn and stained with mud—either that or they were missing altogether—and my mother complained of finding dried-up worms in my trouser pockets.

My father was a fly fisherman, which probably meant that I had both a genetic and cultural predisposition toward fly fishing. It also meant that just as soon as I was old enough to begin mastering some of the rudimentary mechanics of the sport, I became a fly fisherman too—or at least I fished with a fly, which to me was the same thing. After that my father and I sought trout together as often as we could, though it never seemed often enough to me. A serious leg injury had made it all but impossible for him to wade rivers, so we fished mostly from boats in the numerous trout lakes of the Northwest. Our favorites were the famous Kamloops trout lakes of British Columbia, which were then near their best and not far from our home.

For us, in fact, the Kamloops trout became the be-all and end-all of fish, and virtually all our fishing time and attention was soon devoted to it. We knew little of other species. The brown trout was rare in Northwest waters, and in any case all that we had heard or read about it led us to believe that the brown trout was far too polite and fastidious to be considered in the same league as the brawling Kamloops. The rainbow and cutthroat were far more familiar because both were indigenous to our local streams and lakes; they had their good points, but we considered them mostly as fish to practice on in preparation for doing battle with the Kamloops.

Of course we also had heard of steelhead, which were reported to fill many local streams in winter and a few in summer as well, but my father's bad leg kept us from trying to verify the rumors about the incredible size and strength of these fish. Besides, those were just rumors; people talked about steelhead, but I didn't know anybody who ever actually had seen or caught one.

Steelhead stories, it seemed to me, were like cougar stories; people said there were cougars in the woods, and once I had heard the scream of an animal that sounded like what I had imagined a cougar would sound like. But I hadn't seen it or any other one, and again I didn't know anybody who ever had. To me cougars were merely another local legend, a kind of tall tale that people enjoyed telling small boys to make their eyes grow big.

Then one day someone shot a cougar in the woods near town and brought it in and hung it on display in the main street with a sign noting that it measured nine feet from nose to tip of tail. Here at last was tangible evidence that cougars actually existed, evidence I could reach out and touch if I wanted to (although I didn't), and for me cougars passed instantly from the realm of myth to that of reality.

But there was still no evidence at hand to prove the reality of steelhead and I remained skeptical about whether steelhead stories were based on fact or were simply part of an elaborate ruse, a sort of collective joke, like Sasquatch tales, that everybody shared and enjoyed.

Then one day an older cousin told me he actually had caught a steelhead and offered to take me with him next time he went fishing so I could see for myself. I remained skeptical, but this seemed like a chance to get to the heart of the matter, so I quickly agreed to go. On the appointed morning my mother made certain I was bundled up in my heaviest clothing, and my cousin and I set off together for the Nooksack River, which flowed north and east of town.

When we got there he took a stout rod from the trunk of his car and baited up with salmon eggs in a cheesecloth bag, a smelly, messy combination that made me feel slightly queasy. Then he attached a heavy lead sinker to his leader and cast the whole mess out into the slate-colored glacial waters of the Nooksack, propped up his rod in a forked stick and sat back to await developments.

There were no developments. We waited for several hours on the muddy bank while I grew chilly and restless, with nothing more to do than scratch pictures in the soft mud and watch that propped-up rod, which remained as motionless as the skeletal cottonwoods that bordered the river. Finally my cousin took mercy, reeled in the stinking bait, broke down his rod, and we drove home with the car heater on full blast. And despite his assurances that he had previously caught one, I remained as unconvinced as ever about the existence of steelhead.

As I grew older my father's career as an Army officer took him more and more frequently to places far from home, usually to areas of the world considered too dangerous or unstable for the rest of the family to follow. That meant I was often left alone to pursue my piscatorial education, with occasional assistance from my cousin or one of my uncles.

This was a frustrating time, for it meant fewer trips to the fabled Kamloops trout waters and more time spent in pursuit of the smaller, easier, and less-rewarding trout in local streams and lakes. Nevertheless, while most other boys spent their weekends working on cars or doting on girls, I spent most of mine searching for trout. And although the results often were disappointing or lacking altogether, I still found myself learning more about fish and fishing all the time—and perhaps much more about myself as well.

I also read everything about fishing I could lay hands on, both from my father's small collection of angling books and the scarcely larger collection available at the local public library. Among my father's books was a copy of Zane Grey's *Tales of Fresh-Water Fishing*, and I read repeatedly Grey's lurid accounts of fishing for steelhead in Deer Creek, which wasn't far from where I lived, or in Oregon's Rogue River, which seemed like a river of legend.

There was nothing in these tales that contradicted what little I had heard about steelhead; indeed, Grey's descriptions of struggles between man and fish seemed to raise the level of the contest to epic proportions. Grey emerged as a sort of fearless Siegfried, armed only with a fragile fly rod, and the steelhead were fire-breathing dragons of limitless strength. It all seemed much beyond anything I might ever be capable of doing, and I suppose I thought that if the stories were true at all, then catching a steelhead was something that would have to be consigned to that shadowy realm of things that are always left for others to do— like climbing Mount Everest or running a four-minute mile.

Also among my father's books was a well-worn copy of Roderick Haig-Brown's classic *A River Never Sleeps*, and this too I read repeatedly. Haig-Brown's accounts of steelhead fishing were vivid and graceful and less given to outrageous hyperbole, and his writing also conveyed a strong sense of angling ethics that I tried eagerly to grasp as far as I could then understand it. But even in his careful and beautiful prose I found little that seemed to make the steelhead more accessible to a teenaged fisherman whose primary mode of transportation was still a bicycle. Even later, when I learned to drive, I seldom took the family car much farther than the nearest trout lake.

Then came four years of college and two years as a Navy officer, during which time the only fish I saw were schools of flying fish gliding gracefully just beyond the curve of white water at the bow of an aircraft carrier. After six fishless years I headed for Seattle with a new wife and a new job as a newspaper reporter, and it was only then that I began to have the time or means to think once more of fishing.

My father had passed away while I was in college, but I still had his old fly rods together with my own. Even in their cloth cases they had grown musty from so many years of disuse, but all were still serviceable, as were the flies we had put away carefully in plastic containers after our last trip together years before. Soon I began adding to the collection of tackle and learned to tie flies on my own.

I suppose it was natural that when I resumed fishing it was once again for Kamloops trout, since they were the fish I had grown up with and knew best. The Kamloops held most of my attention for the next decade, even serving as the inspiration for a book, and for me it was still the best of all trout.

But during that decade I also began to make the acquaintance of older, more experienced fly fishermen, men such as Ralph Wahl, Enos Bradner, Frank Headrick and Walt Johnson, whose angling reputations were grand enough to inspire near-reverence in one so young as I was then. Most of those reputations had been acquired on steelhead rivers, and I envied them for that; by then I was no longer in doubt as to the existence of steelhead, although I still never had seen one, and mentally I still relegated steelhead fly fishing to a level of skill that I could never hope to attain.

I listened to them talk about steelhead fishing in terms that

were mostly cryptic, and watched them exchange knowing looks that gave evidence of a common experience in which I had never shared. They made it all seem difficult and mysterious, as fly fishermen often do whenever they describe any aspect of the sport to a newcomer, and it seemed to me there was a strong suggestion in everything they said that fly fishing for steelhead was something most ordinary mortals could never hope to learn.

In spite of that, or perhaps because of it, the idea of taking a steelhead on the fly began for me to take on more the aspect of a challenge than an impossible dream; it became my personal Mount Everest, my own four-minute mile.

So I began to try. I'm a stubborn sort, one who believes the best way to find out about something is to do it by one's self, that asking for help is tantamount to acknowledging weakness or ignorance. So it was by myself that I approached my first steelhead river, underequipped and lacking all knowledge of what I was about to try.

I had heard that in steelhead fishing one must forget everything he has learned about trout because steelhead are different both in preference and behavior, and with that dubious advice in mind the river was a complete puzzle to me. I knew where it was likely to hold trout, but not steelhead; I knew how to present the fly so that a trout would be likely to take it, but not a steelhead. Beyond a vague notion culled from the pages of outdoor magazines that steelhead had a disposition for large and brightly colored flies, I did not even know what fly to use. My wading skills were minimal and I was not even certain where to wade or how to control the long casts it was necessary to make across currents of varying speed. Not surprisingly, I caught nothing.

At first I did not try very hard. The lack of success was discouraging, and even though I had learned by then that fishing is enjoyable enough to be worthwhile even when there are no fish to be caught, there were limits to my patience. I would fish a few hours and when nothing happened I would go off somewhere else and fish for trout, which I knew I had a better chance of catching.

Things went on this way for several seasons, during which I

learned very little. But the law of averages was on my side and one day it rewarded me with a quick hookup to a summer steelhead in the Kalama River. It came in the form of a sudden wrenching strike and the quick sight of a flashing silver shape out in the current; but then just as quickly the fish was gone. I know now it was an accident—I had hooked the fish in a patch of quiet water where a steelhead normally would not be found—but it was the first encouragement I'd had.

Not long after that I hooked another fish, this one in the North Fork of the Stillaguamish. It happened in late evening and I fought the fish for nearly half an hour in the fading light. The tired fish was almost within my grasp when the hook pulled out and it swam wearily away. Its loss was hard to bear.

I don't remember now quite how it happened, but I suppose I mentioned these experiences to my new friends Ralph Wahl and Enos Bradner, and I was surprised and pleased when they responded by inviting me to accompany them on a steelhead fishing trip. I never would have thought of asking them for help, but when the overture came from them I was only too eager to respond. It was the beginning of a revelation that, despite what I had earlier mistaken for clannishness and reticence, they were only too willing to share their knowledge of steelhead fly fishing with a newfound friend.

We went together to the Wind River in southwest Washington and scrambled down a steep cliff to fish the Rock Pool, which Bradner had fished for more than twenty years and made famous in his book *Northwest Angling,* and after that we fished the "Holy Water" on the Kalama, a stretch named by steelheaders for its beauty and its abundance of steelhead. As it happened we caught no fish on that trip—although I remember that Ralph fought a fish in the Kalama for quite a while before he lost it— but I learned more during that long weekend than I had in nearly five seasons of fishing by myself.

One could not have asked for two better instructors. Both were world-class steelhead fly fishermen, both wise and experienced and patient and skilled. We soon made other trips together, and once I joined Bradner and Joe Pierce, another skilled and veteran angler, to explore the North Fork of the Toutle and its bright little tributary, the Green River, flowing down from the hills north of glacier-capped Mount St. Helens.

But it was Ralph who finally guided me to my first steelhead on the fly. He took me to the spot, told me what fly to use and exactly where to cast, and cautioned me to be prepared when I did so. His advice was sound in all respects, for when I followed instructions a steelhead suddenly was there, it had my fly in its mouth, it was jumping and running and my reel was answering with a shrill clatter— and then the fish was mine. To be sure, it was a small steelhead, but it was fat and bright and full of the strength that comes only from ocean feeding. And before the day was out, fishing under Ralph's careful instruction, I had released another fish twice as large as the first and broken yet another on a wild unchecked run into a logjam.

Thereafter Ralph and Enos were my tutors, though it was an informal relationship and I am not sure even now if either of them realized I considered them such. They were remarkably different men—Ralph always calm and quiet and thoughtful, Enos always outspoken, opinionated and demonstrative. Their approach to steelhead fishing was equally different; Ralph always was more analytical in his assessment of what was likely to be going on in and under the surface of the river, of how best to approach a suspected steelhead lie and where to place the fly. Brad was more instinctive, relying mostly on experience and intuition in everything he did. Ralph always explained what he was doing, while Bradner taught unconsciously, by example. Their contrasting styles and methods complemented one another and I learned from both.

With their help I began to acquire the necessary skill, but having yet to catch a steelhead by myself I was still lacking in confidence. That, I knew, would come only with success; but success remained elusive until one bright August morning.

I remember it had rained the night before and the woods were still wet as I walked through them toward the hollow rushing sound of the river. I came out on a high bank overlooking the pool I had planned to fish and stood blinking for a moment in the bright dappled sunlight until my eyes adjusted and I saw to my relief there were no other fishermen in the pool.

The water, when I stepped into it, felt cool through the thin waders. The fly rod seemed alive and weightless in my hand as I began to cast. The mint-colored line stabbed far out across the plain of the river and dropped the little dark fly over deep water that I knew hid massive boulders down below.

I remember feeling a fragile sense of hope balanced heavily by the bleak knowledge that I had fished this pool for several seasons without ever hooking a fish, that I still had never landed a steelhead by myself, and the return of those nagging thoughts kindled fresh feelings of self-doubt. So my surprise and disbelief were all the more intense when after only a few casts I felt a sudden swift pull and the surface of the river parted suddenly to reveal a leaping, silver-bright steelhead. The fish fell back with a crash, then turned and raced downriver with line following noisily from my reel.

If you ever have hooked a steelhead you know now what I felt then—a sudden great breath-robbing surge of adrenalin and a sensation very much akin to panic. For a moment I stood paralyzed and could think of nothing else to do but hold the rod high while the fish took out a dangerous length of line. But then the fish stopped and jumped a second time, higher than the first, and the sight of it suddenly snapped me into action. I stumbled out of the river and began running downstream after the fish, scrambling awkwardly over tumbled rocks, threatening roots and cluttered flotsam, all adding to a desperate fear that I would trip and fall or make some other mistake that would cost me the fish.

The steelhead had paused in its flight, perhaps to rest and regain its strength, and that gave me a chance to make up most of the distance and recover much of the line it had taken from me. I tightened up on it and the fish ran again, but this time the run was shorter and I halted it easily and sensed the struggle turning my way. I reeled in slowly and the fish followed grudgingly until I could see the light glinting from its side as it twisted and turned against the relentless pressure of the long rod. Then suddenly it was lying at my feet in the thin water at the margin of the river, its gills opening and closing in the sporadic rhythm of exhaustion, sunlight gleaming from every individual scale as if it were a polished diamond: My first steelhead on the fly.

Thinking now of that day, I am surprised to realize how many years ago it was. Since then many more steelhead have come to my fly in many different waters under many different circumstances, but none has been quite so satisfying as the first. It was with that fish that I finally reached the peak of my personal Everest, broke the time of my private four-minute mile, and I knew then that other successes were bound to follow.

Much later I realized something else: On that long-ago August day I also became a survivor of the process of natural selection that chooses among anglers as surely as it does among steelhead. I had passed through the gantlet of distractions, uncertainties, discouragements and doubts, survived my own stubbornness, failures and lack of confidence, and beaten the longest odds to become a steelhead fly fisherman.

And I have been one ever since.

# 2 | What's in a Name?

I HAVE always thought a fisherman should want to know as much as possible about the fish he seeks—about its life history, its appearance, its behavior and preferences, its habitat and migrations. Such knowledge is rewarding in and of itself, but it also has great practical value; it helps to make one a more efficient and effective fisherman, and it adds immeasurably to the pleasure of the sport.

Yet it requires a considerable investment of effort, time and patience to gain a thorough understanding of even a single species. For me the study of steelhead—which I have always considered a necessary and natural part of my education as a steelhead angler—has meant spending a great deal of time in libraries, poring over books and technical papers, or engaging in discourse with biologists and ecologists who have devoted their lives to the study of fish and their surroundings.

It also has meant spending much time on the rivers, with fly rod temporarily set aside, in observation of the movements of both the water and the fish. It has meant going up to the headwaters in late winter to see the fish in their spawning, or watching in hatcheries as the miracle of their life begins. Some people are unwilling or unable to do all this, but I have always found such activities almost as pleasant and interesting as fishing itself.

The steelhead has many virtues that make it worth studying. The most obvious of these is its physical beauty. A steelhead freshly returned to the river is clean and lithe, a perfectly sculptured streamlined form, and it still wears the colors of the sea— the gunmetal gray of the North Pacific on its back, the gleaming brightness of sunlit waves and broken whitecaps on its sides. After some days or weeks in the river it begins to lose some of this luster and takes on instead the more familiar but scarcely less attractive coloration of the rainbow trout, marked mostly by a gradual reddening of its flanks. This coloration has been described variously as a blush of rose, a strawberry stripe, or a sunset glow, and all these terms are suggestive of its beauty.

Only when the steelhead is at or near spawning does it lose its beauty, and then it becomes dark and ruddy with split and ragged fins and an exaggerated kype in the male fish. But even then it retains something of a quality of nobility.

The strength of the steelhead is another obvious virtue. Stored in its tissues is the latent energy gained in a year or more of feeding in the great ocean—strength enough to drive it on a long passage upstream against all the accumulated weight and momentum of runoff from rainfall, snowmelt, and decaying glaciers. It is this great determined strength that makes the steelhead such an angler's prize, a challenge to test the skill and stamina of the most experienced fisherman.

There is also in the steelhead's life history a great deal that is emotionally appealing to man. A steelhead's existence is a continual contest for survival against long odds, a lonely trial of courage and endurance, and these are the very qualities that men prize most among themselves. They see in the steelhead an exaggerated allegory of their own lives, and I suspect it is this perhaps most of all that has prompted some men to treat the steelhead with a sort of mystical awe that sometimes borders on reverence.

Yet for all the adulation it inspires, the steelhead suffers from a popular name that is not very flattering. By itself, the word "steel" applies very aptly to the color of a fresh-run fish, but when combined with the word "head" it results in a term that clearly suggests a thick-skulled, dim-witted creature. This is unfortunate, for although no trout is a mental giant—they are all creatures of instinct, incapable of anything approaching original thought or reason—the steelhead is certainly no more or less intelligent than any of its relatives.

I have always been curious about the origin of this unflattering name, and also curious why so few other writers appear to have wondered about it. I know of only one other who has asked the question—Trey Combs in his fine little book *The Steelhead Trout*—and his research led him to the same frustrating conclusion as mine: The exact origin of the term remains elusive and obscure both in time and place, although it appears to have been in common usage all along the Pacific Coast well before the end of the nineteenth century. In its original context it also appears to have been more a reference to the thick skull bones of an adult steelhead, which made it a difficult fish to kill with a club, than to any suggested lack of intelligence.

It seems likely that the exact origin of the name may never be known, and today it is in such widespread use—along the Great Lakes tributaries where steelhead have been transplanted as well as throughout their native Pacific coastal range—that it is accepted unquestioningly and seems unlikely to change.

But if the steelhead's common name is firmly established, its scientific name has undergone several changes, and there is still debate over exactly where the steelhead fits in the general taxonomic scheme of things. This is due partly to past confusion over the anadromous and nonanadromous forms of the rainbow trout and to more recent confusion over the complex and often overlapping relationships of steelhead with both Atlantic and Pacific salmon.

Dr. Meredith Gairdner, a physician and naturalist employed by the Hudson's Bay Company, apparently was the first to recognize the steelhead as a distinct species. While at Fort Vancouver in 1833, Gairdner collected steelhead smolts from the Columbia River and sent them, along with his notes, to Sir John Richardson, a leading English naturalist of the time. Three years later Richardson published his *Fauna Boreali Americana*, which included a description of Dr. Gairdner's trout. Richardson classified it as a member of the genus *Salmo*, which already included the Atlantic salmon (*Salmo salar*) and brown trout (*Salmo trutta*), and gave it the specific name *Salmo gairdneri* in honor of its discoverer.

From the beginning it seems to have been understood that the steelhead was an anadromous species, though its differing size and appearance at different stages of its life cycle continued to cause public confusion over its identity. There was also a good deal of scientific confusion, which grew worse in 1855 when Dr. William P. Gibbons captured some trout from San Leandro Creek, California, noted their vivid rainbow colors, and named them *Salmo iridea*. That name later was changed to *Salmo irideus* by the noted taxonomist David Starr Jordan.

The two names—*S. gairdneri* and *S. irideus*—coexisted until late in the nineteenth century, with the first generally applied to the anadromous steelhead and the second to resident rainbow trout. But by the 1890s biologists were beginning to understand that the two fish were actually one and the same, and the names only recognized differing stages in their life cycle. So, following the rules of international taxonomic nomenclature, the earlier name—*S. gairdneri*—was given precedence, and that was how the steelhead was known among the scientific community at least until the early 1960s.

By then further research had revealed evidence that the steelhead and its close cousin, the cutthroat, were both more distantly related to the parent genus *Salmo* than had been thought previously. It also indicated that the steelhead had evolved from the more primitive cutthroat and that Pacific salmon in turn had evolved from steelhead. This led to the suggestion that steelhead and cutthroat should both be reclassified in a subgenus to be known as *Parasalmo*, recognizing their long evolutionary separation from the parent *Salmo*.

The reclassification was not at first universally accepted by taxonomists, but over the years it gained more and more adherents as increasingly sophisticated methods of research began to clarify the complex evolutionary and genetic relationships among the Atlantic salmon (which is actually a trout), the steelhead and cutthroat, and the more recently evolved Pacific salmon.

This debate reached a climax in June 1988 at a meeting of the American Society of Ichthyologists and Herpetologists, where scientists considered a paper presented by Gerald R. Smith and Ralph F. Stearley of the University of Michigan. The paper summarized the long history of taxonomic confusion over the classification of trout and salmon, then presented a case for reclassification of the Pacific trouts. It argued that biochemical, morphological and ecological evidence indicated a clear evolutionary trend among salmonid fish from strictly freshwater forms, such as the grayling and the Siberian lenok, to levels of "intermediate anadromy," such as the chars, to increasing loss of dependence on fresh water, such as in steelhead and the more advanced Pacific salmon, *Oncorhynchus.*

It also argued that one of the characteristics that always had been cited as a primary difference between steelhead and Pacific salmon—the fact that steelhead can survive after spawning, whereas salmon cannot—was in reality not as clear-cut as had been supposed. The paper pointed out that only a small percentage of steelhead survive after spawning, and that at least one species of Pacific salmon, *Oncorhynchus masou,* the so-called cherry salmon of Japan, has races in which some individuals *do* survive after spawning. In both cases, Smith and Stearley said, the "mechanism of death appears to be highly similar . . . involving rapid senescence due to accelerated pituitary and adrenal activity."

In summary, the paper said, "the pattern of the gradation between trouts and salmons argues against separation of Pacific trouts as a separate genus. The distribution of morphological, biochemical and ecological character states shows a primitive group, trouts, whose anadromous forms are salmon-like, and an advanced group, salmon, the earliest members of which are trout-like."

On the basis of that evidence, and after considering several alternatives, Smith and Stearley recommended that the cutthroat, steelhead, rainbow, and other forms of Pacific Basin trout—the Apache, Gila, golden and Mexican golden trouts— should all be lumped together with the Pacific salmon in the same genus, *Oncorhynchus.* "This classification has the advantage of reflecting true historical relationships and evolutionary trends," they concluded.

But the steelhead-rainbow still presented a special case. The paper acknowledged evidence that the steelhead of the Pacific coast of North America and *Salmo mykiss*, the Kamchatka trout of the Soviet Union, are genetically virtually indistinct—in other words, they are the same fish. The Kamchatka trout received its specific name in 1792 from the naturalist Johanne Walbaum, and since the rules of nomenclature require that the earliest name be given precedence, Smith and Stearley argued that *mykiss* should be applied to both the Asian and North American forms of the steelhead-rainbow. Hence the steelhead would go from *Salmo gairdneri* to *Oncorhynchus mykiss*.

Those recommendations were accepted, and early in 1989 the American Fisheries Society's Committee on Names of Fishes formally established *Oncorhynchus* as the new generic name for western trouts and *Oncorhynchus mykiss* as the new specific name for the steelhead.

It is tempting to say—and only half facetiously—that it's easy to see how an organization calling itself the American Society of Ichthyologists and Herpetologists would have little compunction about changing a time-honored, smooth, and esthetically pleasing name like *Salmo* to an awkward, clunky, tongue-sticking name like *Oncorhynchus*. Of course, the scientists agreed to the change for what they no doubt felt were good and worthwhile reasons, but one cannot help but wish that anglers also had been given a vote. The fact is that for every similarity cited by scientists between Pacific salmon and steelhead, anglers can cite a difference—and those differences are important enough, at least from a fisherman's point of view, to forever hold salmon and steelhead separate and apart, no matter what their evolutionary history.

Perhaps the most obvious of these differences is that steelhead remain bright and strong long after they return to the rivers, and thus remain desirable to catch, while most salmon returning to fresh water quickly turn rusty and ugly and break out with the blotches of fungus that make them look like piscatorial lepers.

Another obvious difference is in the timing of the runs; it is possible to find steelhead in the rivers every month of the year, though the heaviest runs are in winter throughout most of the steelhead's Pacific coastal range. The timing of salmon runs, on the other hand, is much more discrete, and after January, when the last spawned-out chum has died, the rivers are empty of salmon at least until spring.

The relative fecundity of the two is another big difference. Steelhead always have been much less numerous than salmon and therefore are more highly prized by anglers who seek both species. Steelhead and salmon also display far different preferences in the types of water they choose in rivers; the steelhead likes swifter, shallower water, which is always much more interesting to fish than the deep, quiet pools frequented by most salmon.

But perhaps the most important difference of all is the salmon's unwillingness under most circumstances to take an artificial fly, or its unwillingness under nearly all circumstances to take a dry fly, while the steelhead is wondrously responsive to both. From a fisherman's viewpoint, nothing could distinguish the two more strikingly than that.

Aside from all this, it also seems apparent that the scientists who agreed to the name change did not consider what a nightmare of confusion they were creating for the common vernacular. They have left us a situation in which the Atlantic salmon, a true trout, is still called a salmon in common parlance, while the steelhead—which always before has been classified as a trout—is now to be called a Pacific salmon in the scientific jargon. Nothing could be more confusing than that.

It won't work, of course, and most people probably will go on referring to the Atlantic salmon as a salmon and to the steelhead as a trout, and eventually even the scientific community probably will have to revisit the issue, if only to try to resolve the confusion.

Not that there was unanimous agreement over the name change in the first place. Some biologists and geneticists still think that the differences in life history, habits, and physical characteristics between Pacific salmon and steelhead are great enough to warrant some taxonomic distinction between them, perhaps at least in the form of subgenus classification for the steelhead. Something of the sort would seem like a logical solution to the nomenclatural dilemma we now face.

Not that it really makes any difference to fishermen in the long run. The steelhead by any other name is still a steelhead, and no change in nomenclature can make it otherwise.

All steelhead spawn in late winter or early spring. Even summer fish that may enter the rivers in May or June will wait until the following January or February or even later before spawning. Their eggs hatch in April, May, or later, and when their yolk sacs are absorbed the alevins will emerge from the gravel and go about the business of feeding and growing.

Steelhead hatched in the rivers of California and southern Oregon take less time to grow to smolting size than their northern counterparts, probably a consequence of the warmer water temperatures and longer growing seasons of the southern rivers, and they may migrate to sea after only a year or two in fresh water and return after only a single season of ocean feeding—small but game fish like the famous "half-pounders" of Oregon's Rogue River.

Fish hatched in the rivers of northern Oregon and Washington usually take two years to reach smolting size, and here as elsewhere there appears to be a curious correlation between time spent in the river and time spent at sea—these fish often return to their native rivers only after two years of feeding at sea, by which time they will have reached a weight of six to ten pounds.

In the colder climate of British Columbia and southern Alaska it is not uncommon for young steelhead to spend three years in the rivers before their first migration, and they may spend three or even four years at sea before returning to spawn. This accounts for the very large fish in such famous British Columbia rivers as the Dean, Babine, Kispiox, and Thompson.

So the farther north one goes, the older and larger adult steelhead tend to be. Spring and summer steelhead runs also are more

common in the north, and some northern rivers host runs of both summer and winter fish. The universal requirement for a summer run seems to be a river with a good sustained cold summer flow, which usually means a river with shaded canyon reaches or heavy timber along its shores. This makes summer steelhead rivers especially vulnerable to logging, and many runs have been damaged or destroyed when the dense timber stands along the riverbanks have been stripped away.

Though summer and winter runs of steelhead may share the same river, they somehow remain reproductively isolated from each other. In other words, summer fish spawn only with those of their own kind and winter fish do likewise, so there is no danger of crossbreeding that might upset the genetic programming that determines run timing in both races.

The majority of steelhead runs occur in relatively short-run coastal rivers, but some steelhead penetrate far inland—notably those ascending the Fraser and Columbia rivers and their tributaries. And these long-distance runners do not appear to be cut from exactly the same cloth as their coastal counterparts. The most visible difference is in their scale counts, which are higher, and in the scales themselves, which are smaller than those of coastal fish. The inland fish also tend to have fewer spots, and smaller ones, than coastal steelhead, and also may vary in coloration. These and other differences have led some biologists to conclude that the fish of the upper Fraser and Columbia river drainages may represent a separate species or subspecies. Dr. Robert J. Behnke of Colorado State University has proposed the name "redband trout" for these fish.

These geographical trends and differences among steelhead are relatively easy to observe and describe, but they are really nothing much more than informed generalizations, and for each of them there is likely to be at least one exception. What may be true of fish in one watershed does not necessarily always hold true for fish in the next, and steelhead are justifiably famous for their unpredictability.

Not a great deal is known of the steelhead's behavior at sea. Those fish that return after only a single season obviously do not travel far, but those that spend two or more years at sea are known to venture great distances to the north and west. A fourteen-pound steelhead caught in Washington's Nisqually River on April 14, 1988, had been tagged and released by Japanese researchers on June 19, 1987, at a location near the international date line several hundred miles south of Adak, Alaska—and more than twenty-five hundred miles from the Washington coast. It was the first time since tagging operations began in 1956 that a Puget Sound steelhead had been documented west of 155 degrees west longitude. A thirty-one-inch steelhead captured in Washington's Sol Duc River on March 12, 1989, had traveled even farther—it was tagged thirty-seven hundred miles from home. Close behind was a fish tagged in April 1987 as an outmigrant steelhead at the Quinault Indian Tribe's Lake Quinault rearing station and caught June 23, 1989, by a Japanese research ship in the Western Pacific, 3,603 miles away.

These are only a few of many examples of well-traveled steelhead. Their migratory routes evidently follow temperature gradients influenced by seasonal changes and fluctuations in ocean currents. They feed on targets of opportunity, mostly krill and small fish. The duration of their journeys is governed by the timing of sexual maturation, which triggers the urge to turn toward home.

Just exactly how they know where home is remains another mystery, though theories abound; what is known is that once they do reach the proximity of their home river, their keen olfactory sense takes over and plays a large role in getting them to the right destination.

But they do not always return unerringly to the river of their birth; examples of "strayed" steelhead are relatively common. This appears to happen occasionally even under normal circumstances, but natural disasters appear to exacerbate the rate of straying. For example, after the 1980 explosion of Mount St. Helens, which filled the Toutle River with mudflows and made it virtually impassable to steelhead, an unusual number of Toutle River summer steelhead turned up in the Kalama River, the next watershed south.

Upon arrival in the estuary off the mouth of its home river, a steelhead may wait for a combination of high tide and freshet to provide easy entry to the stream. However, this is probably more often true of small streams than larger ones, where the streamflow usually is sufficient to allow entry at any time. Once in the river, a steelhead may travel upstream as much as eight miles a day, usually avoiding heavy water and following the path of least resistance. Most of this movement takes place in early morning or early evening hours—traditionally good times for fishing.

Summer steelhead move upstream until they find a safe "staging" area—a place with cool, well-oxygenated water and cover to provide security from predators—and there they settle down to wait until dislodged by fall or winter freshets, when they will move on to seek secure resting spots near their spawning grounds. Winter fish are more direct in their behavior; they move upstream rapidly to their spawning grounds, and usually not many weeks will pass before they are spawning. Summer fish therefore are available to anglers for a much longer time, and usually under water conditions that are much more conducive to fly fishing.

The question of whether steelhead feed in fresh water has long been debated. Their entry into the river is accompanied by physiological changes that include atrophy of the digestive system, and they live mostly off stored fats. Yet unquestionably some do feed, although rarely do they do so in a deliberate or consistent fashion. Even winter fish are known to feed, though food is scarce in winter and feeding behavior is much more common among summer steelhead. Occasionally in late summer one will see a steelhead rise consistently to floating grasshoppers or hatching mayflies, though such occurrences are rare; much more likely is a single spur-of-the-moment feeding response that is not repeated.

Some anglers have theorized that this is a memory response—that when confronted with something it recognizes as edible, a steelhead may respond involuntarily out of deep-seated habit. The late Enos Bradner had a different theory; he reasoned that the steelhead is a naturally curious creature, and lacking hands or fingers to feel things, it does the only other thing it can—takes them into its mouth to examine them.

Whatever the reason, the feeding response *does* occur—and anglers can be thankful for it.

Yet it does not occur predictably. In contrast to the feeding response of a resident rainbow trout, which is at least somewhat dependable, a steelhead's behavior is never certain. In a way they are like young men who have gone off to war and have been forever changed by the experience in ways that no one else can understand. Perhaps that is what happens to steelhead when they go off on their long journeys through the perils of the twilight sea; they return changed to rivers that are unchanged, and they do not know quite how to behave—nor do we know fully what to expect of them.

But there are still times when a steelhead will revert at least temporarily to the behavior pattern of the trout it always has been—and deep down still is—and rise swiftly to a floating fly or turn to chase a drifting nymph. Perhaps Roderick Haig-Brown said it best: "The steelhead is not a very discriminating fish, but he is extremely capricious." It is that capriciousness that makes it possible to cast a fly thirty times over a resting steelhead without eliciting a flicker of response—and then, on the thirty-first cast, the fish may suddenly come to the fly with a great rush.

The steelhead also is secretive in its ways. You may catch sight of one rolling in the pale evening light or see the brief shifting shape of one deep in a translucent pool, but in most rivers you will not see them often and you will never see them well. Sometimes you must take it largely on faith that they are there, concealed in the depths or hidden by the writhing current. But you may never know for sure until one takes your fly.

The steelhead is and always will remain an elusive, enigmatic quarry, and steelhead fishing is largely a matter of being in the right place at the right time and doing the right thing. The first two of these are mostly matters of luck, although the element of chance can be much reduced through observation and experience. But doing the right thing is wholly a matter of skill, which can be acquired, and persistence also raises the odds for success.

So it is possible to learn much about steelhead and still not know very much about them. But that is one of the great charms of steelhead fishing; the more you learn about it, the more you realize how much more there is to learn. Books and research and observation can and do contribute much to the knowledge and success of a steelhead angler, but in the final analysis the most valuable and vivid lessons are those that can only be learned out on the rivers, from the steelhead itself.

# 3 | ON THE DESCHUTES

I WAS dreaming that I had hooked an absurdly fat, balloon-shaped pig of a fish that improbably had risen from the water and was now circling around me in the air, darting up and down like a child's kite in a gusting breeze. Then the alarm clock went off and I awoke to the equally absurd reality that it was only three o'clock in the morning, that I had been in bed less than two hours, and that I was in a very dark motel room in Hoods River, Oregon.

Only one thing could have been responsible for such a set of circumstances: Steelhead.

Through the thin wall I could hear thumping and bumping in the next room that told me my friend Alan Pratt was already up and getting his gear together. We had driven down from Seattle the day before to meet Dan Stair, who through arrangement with a mutual friend was to take us in his jet boat up the Deschutes River to fish for steelhead.

Dan worked for a tackle-manufacturing company in a sort of vaguely defined job as combination field-tester/public-relations man, which meant he spent most of his time either fishing, taking other people fishing, or talking about fishing. He seemed undisturbed that we planned to fish with flies, which his company didn't sell, and not with lures, which it did. In fact he seemed generally undisturbed by much of anything; his whole attitude and appearance—he was a short, dark, powerfully built man—suggested he would have been just as comfortable with the idea if we had decided we wanted to go down to the river and take turns wrestling one-on-one with a sturgeon instead of fishing for steelhead.

He also proved to be a most cordial host and the three of us had sat up eating, drinking, and talking fishing far into the night, all of which had undoubtedly contributed to my crazy dream about the balloon-shaped flying fish.

But now it was only moments before Dan was scheduled to pick us up and take us to the river, so I stumbled out of bed, switched on the light, and tried to synchronize the commands issuing from my groggy mind with the movements of my limbs while I groped for my clothing and my gear.

By the time everything was together and I had splashed some cold water on my face in an effort to get my eyes to open a little wider, Dan was waiting outside in his Jeep, jet sled in tow. It was still quite dark, but the twenty-foot sled with its twin eighty-horsepower outboard jets and its skeleton trailer gleamed menacingly under a row of mercury-vapor lamps, looking like some ugly giant metallic insect poised to pounce on its prey.

When Al and I and our gear were loaded in the Jeep, Dan pulled onto the interstate and headed east for The Dalles, where the great broad ribbon of the Deschutes breaks out of the Oregon desert to join the Columbia. We rode in silence along the dark, empty interstate. A few hours earlier the three of us had been engaged in convivial, animated conversation, but now it seemed none of us had anything left to say; perhaps we already had gotten to know one another well enough so that no further conversation was necessary.

That certainly was true for Al and me. We had shared many earlier trout-fishing adventures and misadventures together, most notably a memorable trip to Montana when Al had brought along a tape player and a single tape—Mozart's *Eine Kleine Nachtmusik*—which we had played so many times that we could each whistle the complete score from memory by the time we returned home.

Al is a tall, lanky, laid-back sort of person, a newspaper cartoonist by profession and possibly the nearest thing to a genius of anyone I've ever met. His genius is in his humor, which he applies freely and equally to everything and everybody, and if he has a serious bone in his body he keeps it well hidden. This, coupled with a marvelous ability to tell stories, a relentless love for fly fishing and a cultivated fondness for good food, decent cigars, and charcoal-filtered bourbon, makes him the quintessential fishing companion, and I have always been grateful to the piscatorial gods for making us friends—no doubt in a moment of whimsy.

But for all our travels together in search of trout, this was the first time we had ever gone in quest of steelhead. It also was one of the first trips I had made since taking my first unassisted steelhead on the fly, an episode that had given me a new feeling of confidence that I was eager to test on the fish of the Deschutes.

It was still dark when we reached the canyon of the Deschutes. The river was invisible, hidden somewhere in the gloomy depths of the canyon, and only the heavy sound of its passage gave proof of its existence. When we got down to the edge of it the water was as dark as ink, sliding past easily in its well-worn course between the great rock ramparts of the canyon walls, distinguishable now only because their vast bulk blotted out the morning stars on each horizon.

It took some time to launch and load the sled, put on our waders and life jackets and set up our rods, and by the time we were finally ready to go the eastern sky had begun to pale with the first full flush of morning light. Dan got behind the console and turned the starter and the twin jets responded with a deep-throated growl that contended with the sounds of the river. He swung the prow away from the bank and steered the sled out into the center of the flow, where the surface was just beginning to reflect the oncoming light of morning. Then he hit the throttles and the sled leaped forward on a long rising tongue of spray,

skidding swiftly and noisily over dark upwellings and silver scrolls of current as we rushed upstream toward the open maw of the canyon.

The flow of the river had been sluggish where we started but it soon quickened as we hurtled our way upstream until the sled was slamming and sliding over great rips and dips and dimples in the hard-running current and the vague shape of the shoreline was slipping past at what seemed an impossible speed. Soon we came to the first of the many rapids for which the Deschutes is named, a place where the whole great river narrowed itself to squeeze through a few small gaps in a ragged ledge of old lava, forming great tubes and chutes of rushing water, huge standing waves, and wild flying sheets of spray. "Hang on!" Dan shouted, and then his voice was lost in the immense raw noise of angry water and the howl of the straining jets, enormous sounds that beat on our eardrums and thumped in our chests as the sled flew forward into the cauldron of spray. Then just as quickly the rapids were past and we were skimming swiftly over quiet water once again, with cold spray trickling down our faces, laughing at the wild exhilaration of it all.

In such fashion we made our way up the river, running smoothly over broad reaches of even flow separated by harrowing stairsteps of dangerous rock and furious rapid, each appearing more formidable than the one just past.

More and more detail of the canyon's interior became visible as the glow of morning filled the sky. Finally the sun heaved itself over the eastern rim and bathed the opposite wall of the canyon in harsh, relentless light, transforming what had been a vague monolithic shape into vivid three-dimensional colors, forms and textures—tall palisades of rock with stains of crimson, yellow, brown and purple from leached minerals or clinging lichens, giving way below to vast sloping fans of eroded broken rock that reached all the way down to the river. Halfway down the slope a thin layer of dry soil had begun to form atop the broken rubble, just soil enough to support a few stubborn tufts of pale yellow bunch grass and scattered dusty clots of sage. Near the bottom of the canyon next to the river itself the soil was deeper, and scraps of green foliage lined the banks as far up as their roots could find water.

Then there was the river itself, impressively noisy, impressively large, and always impressively strong as we glimpsed it through sheets of spray in the gathering light. The sunlight gave it translucency so that we could see for the first time that the river was carrying the pale gray smoke of snowmelt and glacial runoff from mountains far upstream.

We had gone about a dozen miles upriver before Dan finally eased back on the throttles and steered the sled into a quiet eddy and up to the rocky shore. By then we had grown stiff from holding on tightly to the metal thwarts and our faces were flushed from being pelted by cold spray, but our waders and jackets had kept the rest of us dry—and we were ready and anxious for fishing.

Dan put us on a deep run next to a steep bank with little wading room and we began fishing through it with sinking lines and wet flies while the sun climbed higher and the clear harsh light of early morning gave way to a softer, more diffuse kind of hazy light that reduced the vivid colors of the canyon wall to pastel shades of brown and yellow centered around the great gray ribbon of the river. It was July and we were deep in desert country, but it remained cool on the canyon floor next to the cold river.

The morning was well advanced by the time we had fished through the deep run, and neither Al nor I had moved a fish. Dan suggested it was time to look for greener pastures, so we returned to the boat and spent the next several hours hopscotching up and down the river, stopping to fish in every likely looking run or riffle.

During those travels we saw several other fishermen who either had run up the river in jet sleds, as we had, or had floated down in McKenzie boats; it was necessary to do one or the other to reach this section of the river because the lower Deschutes flows through virtually roadless country and in most places there is no access other than by the river itself. As a member of the vast legion of wading anglers who have been angered at one time or another by the thoughtless behavior of jet-boat pilots, I was glad to see that Dan was careful to give these other fishermen a friendly wave and a wide, throttled-down berth so he would not disturb the water they were fishing.

At one late-morning stop Dan scored our first success by taking a bright ten-pound steelhead on one of his company's lures. But we had no other action and by midafternoon Al and I were still searching for our first fish.

By then we had come to a long drift below an old abandoned railroad water tower, a place where the river broadened and its flow evened out over an undulating bottom of coarse gravel—a striking contrast to the faster runs paved with chunks of razor-sharp shale that we had been fishing most of the day. It was perfect fly-fishing water, with easy wading and plenty of room for long backcasts, and it also seemed to hold a promise of steelhead.

I had fished about halfway through the run when that promise was suddenly fulfilled. A strong fish took my sunken fly with a shock that traveled all the way to my shoulders; before I could react the fish had turned, taken what little slack line I held in my hand, and started off on a wild downstream run. With rod held high and reel running hard, I waded out to follow the fish from shore.

The fish was well into the backing and still going strong by the time I reached the beach. On and on it ran, aided by the swift current, and I could see there would be no easy way to turn it. Fortunately, there were no obstructions in my path and I was able to trot along the rocky beach in pursuit of the fish until it finally stopped of its own accord, just above the tail-out of the long drift. It held there, having spent most of its energy in that impossibly long first run, and I reeled hard as I ran toward it until all of the backing and much of my fly line were back on the reel.

Then the steelhead started off again. The rest of its fight consisted of a series of strong, short rushes, each one stopped and turned more easily than the last, until finally the fish was on its side, exhausted, and I was able to lead it gently to the rocky beach. It was a fine buck steelhead of about seven pounds, thick and bright except for a narrow ribbon of pale rose on either flank, and the power of its first long run had already left an indelible mark on my memory.

That fish, plus the one Dan had taken earlier, were the only ones we caught that day. Late in the afternoon, as the canyon began filling up with shadows, we started back downstream, helped along in our descent by the swift current that now was running with instead of against us. By the time we arrived back in Hood River it was after dark and we were hungry and exhausted, and that evening our fishing talk ended early.

Next morning, after a much better night's sleep, we were back in the water-tower run at first light. We had been fishing only a few minutes—just long enough for the morning chill and the coolness of the river to seep through my waders and jacket and start me shivering—when I felt something that triggered a chill of a different kind: For some reason I knew, beyond the shadow of any doubt, that a fish would take on my very next cast. I could not explain the feeling—cannot explain it to this day, although the same thing has happened to me several times since—but I made the cast with the absolutely certain foreknowledge that I was about to catch a fish.

Sure enough, as the sunken fly swept through its arc I felt a sharp pull and knew that a steelhead had plucked at the fly and missed. A split second later it came again and this time it was firmly hooked. There was no question of taking up slack; the line was taut from the moment of taking and the fish turned swiftly at the first feeling of resistance and ran far out into the middle of the river, then changed direction and headed downstream. It began to jump—once, twice, three times, then again and again until I had counted nine consecutive jumps, all of them high and tumbling, each farther away than the last.

Once again I was compelled to go ashore and follow as the fish kept going downstream until it had run all the way out of the water-tower drift and was headed for a rocky stretch of dangerous-looking broken water down below. It reached the broken stretch and twice took the line around exposed rocks far out in the river, but each time I was able to wade out far enough to throw a loop in the fly line and free it from the obstruction. Then the fish headed down again, jumping twice more, and stopped only when it was out of the run and into a patch of quiet water. It held there long enough for me to catch up with it, out of breath from the long chase.

By then the steelhead's strength was totally spent and I wasn't much better off myself. But I managed to guide the fish to shore and slide it up gently on a little comma-shaped stretch of dark volcanic sand where I stood over it and marveled at its size, which was scarcely more than five pounds. It didn't seem possible that such a small fish could have been so strong, but there was an unmistakable look of strength in every curved line of its body, and the fish was as firm and bright as a polished steel bayonet. Never before, and rarely since, have I fought a fish as wild or as handsome as that one.

It was the start of a memorable day. Not long after I had taken that fish, Al hooked another one near the tail of the water-tower drift and lost it after a long fight when it ran down into the fast water and took his line around a rock farther out than either of us could wade to free it. Then came a lull of several hours, during which we sampled several different runs without success, until at midafternoon Dan dropped us off on a bleached pile of rocks in the middle of the river, a tiny island exposed only during summer low water. Below the rock pile was a long gravel bar that tapered downstream into deep water; the current on one side was too swift to fish with a fly, but on the other a complex series of currents swirled around and past the skeleton of an old tree, offering an intriguing place to fish.

My first cast was seized by one of those complicated currents, which brought the fly back almost to my feet, so I stripped more line from the reel and threw a longer cast quartering upstream. The fly landed in an upwelling of current and hung there, suspended, while another current, closer in, caught the line and drew it downstream in a large curving belly. Suddenly a steelhead charged the suspended fly, took it, and kept going straight up, rocketing out of the river like a missile launched from a submarine. But the belly in the line kept me from setting the hook, and I could see the fly come away even before the fish fell back to the water.

The thing had happened so quickly that it seemed a long time before I felt the familiar stab of disappointment that inevitably comes from a lost fish, but once the feeling came it stayed with me like a bitter aftertaste as I fished through the remainder of the run. When I felt I had exhausted all its possibilities I left it and started wading downstream along the sloping gravel bar, casting as I went, until I had gone down as far as I could without letting the river come in over my wader tops. From that point I began casting downstream, lengthening each cast, hoping to cover as much water beyond wading range as possible. After the third or fourth such cast, just as the fly swung around below me, it was taken by a heavy fish.

The steelhead jumped twice, then started downstream where I could not follow, but I was soon able to turn it and regain most of the line it had taken. For several more minutes we traded line back and forth until the fish began to tire and I was able to get it on a short line and begin the retreat to shallow water where I could beach it. Then suddenly the steelhead ran directly toward me and went right between my legs! Hoping that Al didn't have his camera trained on me, I managed an awkward pirouette and lifted one wader-clad leg over the fly line without falling into the river. In another few moments the fish was safely on the beach and I was admiring it, a bright hen steelhead almost as pretty as the one I had taken earlier, but its sudden maneuver had managed to make me feel foolish and awkward.

That was the last fish of the trip, but the lure of the Deschutes and its steelhead was too powerful to resist, and two months later we were back again. This time we drove down in Al's camper, which we parked on a level sandy spot amid the sagebrush on a hillside overlooking the river near its mouth. Dan met us there the next morning, jet sled once again in tow, and we climbed in for the usual wild ride up the river.

Our first stop once again was the water-tower drift where we had enjoyed so much success on our earlier trip, but now it was September and the water level was much lower than it had been in July. The run seemed empty of fish and once we had spent enough time there to convince ourselves of that we headed farther upstream, beyond where we had gone on the earlier trip, to prospect in unfamiliar waters.

I had enjoyed most of the luck during our July trip, but this time it was Al's turn. He took two fish and lost two others in upstream pools while I went without any action at all until early evening. By then we had started working our way slowly back downstream and had made a last stop to fish a long run of broken water that bordered a great white curving tongue of current at a sharp bend in the river.

Almost at once I had a hard strike from a steelhead that ran from the moment of taking, and in the fast-fading light I could not tell which direction it had gone; all I knew was that my reel was spinning wildly and alarming lengths of line were disappearing into that great roaring tongue of white water and wind-whipped spray.

The run finally ended, but when I took the first tentative answering turns on the reel the line quickly came up tight against a dead, unyielding weight. Somewhere, far out in the angry river, the leader was caught fast on a rock or snag. In the end there was nothing to do but pull until the leader snapped.

All this happened in much less time than it takes to tell about it, and I had never even come close to being in control of the situation. That fish left me feeling badly humbled.

By then it was too late to think of fishing longer, and full darkness had fallen by the time Dan dropped us at the river's edge and we trudged up the hillside to Al's camper. Al went inside and turned on a light and a great horde of tiny gnats swarmed instantly through the open door; by the time he closed it the whole ceiling of the camper was a moving mass of tiny black bugs. They weren't the biting kind, however, so we tried to ignore them as I fetched ice and mixed drinks while Al began tossing a salad for supper. But then gnats began falling into both drinks and salad until they looked as if they had been sprinkled liberally with pepper. We tried using our hats to brush away the pesky little bugs, but each swipe only generated an air current that sent dozens more plummeting into our supper. Gnats swarmed in our faces and crawled in our ears; there were simply too many to cope with, and it was beginning to look as if they might drive us right outside into the cold desert night.

But with his typical resourcefulness, Al soon came up with a solution for the problem. He switched off the light, which had been the main thing to attract the bugs in the first place, and lit a burner on the camper's propane stove. The seductive blue flame of the burner soon drew gnats by the thousand; they orbited around it, flying closer and closer until caught in the rising heat. Then, one by one, they turned to tiny glowing sparks and fell lifeless into the flame.

We sat there sipping our drinks, transfixed by the amazing spectacle that we agreed looked like a recreation of the Battle of Britain on a hopelessly miniature scale. Finally, after the last tiny winged victim had spiraled down in flames, we turned on the light again and enjoyed a peaceful supper.

The next day's fishing was nearly a duplicate of the first. Al took a lovely eight-pound steelhead early on, the largest fish either of us landed on either trip, while I fished the morning long without a touch. But just after noon I cast to a slick below a large boulder in a stretch of deep and difficult water and a steelhead took the fly almost as it touched the water. Characteristically, the fish ran immediately and the water was too deep and fast for me to follow; I could only stay where I was and hold on while more and more backing peeled off the reel. With all the fly line out and most of the backing, the fish was soon beyond control, and somewhere, far out in the trailing ribbons of current, it found a rock, ran the leader around it, and broke off. As before, it was the only fish I hooked all day.

So our second trip to the Deschutes turned out to be a less successful one for me, at least in terms of numbers of fish on the beach. But any trip that includes the companionship of good friends, the exhilarating experience of those turbulent jet-sled rides up and down that magnificent river, and the memory of brief moments of connection with a pair of wild steelhead could hardly be counted as unsuccessful.

I would go again even if I knew in advance that the results would be the same.

# 4 | OBJECTS OF AFFECTION

ONE OF THE many attractions of steelhead fly fishing is in owning the implements used in its practice. Almost without exception, these are things of unique function, feel, and shape, and most have at least as much esthetic appeal as they do utilitarian value. It seems a fisherman never can own enough of them.

First and foremost are the rods, those long, gleaming, slender shafts of cane or glass or graphite that are just as pleasant to hold as to behold. Pick up one of these and you will instantly feel its coiled-up strength, its restless latent energy waiting to be released. Just as quickly you will find yourself admiring its graceful lines, the high gloss of its smooth finish, and the satisfying shape and feel of its springy round cork grip. A good rod is a precision instrument designed and built to be used and admired with the same regard and affection a musician might have for his favorite oboe or violin.

The choice of a rod for steelhead fly fishing—or fly fishing of any kind, for that matter—is almost as complex and personal as choosing a mate. To varying degrees, an angler's choice of rod will reflect his experience, casting style, the size of the rivers he fishes, the type of method he prefers, perhaps even something of his own personality. And, just as in choosing a mate, once an angler makes up his mind on a certain rod he generally will stick with it, come what may. Fly fishermen, above all things, tend to be conservative and traditional in such matters.

But making up one's mind is more of a task today than it was just a few years ago. Back then the choice was limited to rods made of bamboo or fiberglass, and rod weight and strength were much more important considerations than they are now. Now there are also graphite and boron rods to choose from, and the light weight and amazing strength of these materials has freed rodmakers to experiment with new designs that would have been impossible fifteen years ago. That's all to the good, and anglers have benefited greatly from these developments—but the vastly greater selection of different rod designs now available also has made the task of choosing the right one much more complicated.

Another result of these recent technological innovations is a strong trend among manufacturers to produce more very long, very light graphite rods, including more and more double-handed steelhead fly rods in lengths of twelve or fourteen feet or greater. Such rods, traditional on Atlantic salmon rivers of the British Isles, never have been very popular on this side of the Atlantic because they were always made of heavy cane. But now that light graphite models are available, they seem to be catching on rapidly among steelhead fly fishermen, and for some very good reasons. A long rod of any kind, but especially a double-hander, makes longer casts possible, and that in turn allows an angler to cover a large river much more thoroughly and efficiently. A long rod also provides more effective control of line once the cast is made, and greatly simplifies the task of mending. The light weight of graphite or boron allows an angler to handle such a rod through a whole full day of fishing without tiring.

All this I can readily understand and appreciate—and yet my own preference is for smaller rods, rarely more than eight or eight and a half feet for steelhead, sometimes not even that. I simply enjoy the feel of a smaller rod, and although the shorter length imposes some handicaps that could easily be resolved by switching to a longer model, these are things I have willingly chosen to accept. This choice is in keeping with what I conceive to be the whole philosophical basis of fly fishing, which is the self-imposed acceptance of a series of challenges and restrictions, each one calculated to add to the difficulty and complexity that is the essence of the sport.

Not that smaller rods don't offer some advantages of their own. They are far less forgiving than their longer cousins, so they require their users to become masters of the mechanics of casting and more adept at controlling line, and such skills cannot help but make one a better angler. Or perhaps that is just another way of rationalizing the choice I have made.

I suppose it was the well-publicized light-tackle exploits of Lee Wulff and other fishermen in the 1960s that first steered me toward smaller rods. Wulff attracted a lot of attention in the angling world by taking large Atlantic salmon on tiny "midge" rods of six feet or less, and later, in conversation and correspondence, he encouraged me to try similar tackle for steelhead. Further inspiration came from watching Walt Johnson, one of the Northwest's premier steelhead fly fishermen, using a tiny rod on the North Fork of the Stillaguamish. At length I decided to try it myself and to keep on trying until I had landed a steelhead on a midge rod.

The rod I chose for the purpose was one I had built for trout fishing, a six-footer weighing slightly less than two ounces and designed to handle a 6-weight line. It worked well for trout—indeed, a ten- or twelve-inch fish became a whole new experience on such a tiny rod—but when I first tried using it for steelhead I soon found the light rod-and-line combination limited my casting distance on wide-open, windswept rivers. So I began carrying two rods, a longer one to fish open stretches when the wind was blowing, and the little six-footer for use on smaller protected pools.

There was no problem hooking fish with the little rod; in fact, I hooked several before I landed one. The first two were both hooked in a narrow pool where an old dead tree had come to rest with its butt end stuck in the river bottom; the thick shaft of the tree's trunk angled up so that its skeletal upper branches were visible just beneath the surface of the river. I knew from past experience that steelhead liked to rest beneath those spreading branches, a spot from which they could easily be moved to a fly—although those same branches made the pool a very difficult and hazardous place to try to play and land a fish.

The first fish I hooked with the midge rod took the fly on the near side of the sunken tree, plunged directly under the leaning trunk, and exploded out of the water in a tremendous leap on the other side. When I retrieved the slack line I found the leader broken well up near the heavy butt section; the whole episode was over in microseconds.

The second fish took on the far side of the tree and jumped immediately. I snubbed it as hard as I could while it was still off balance from the jump and managed to lead it over the submerged tree to my side of the river. But then the steelhead quickly got the better of things; it started off on a long downstream run that I could not check, and somewhere in the lower reaches of the pool it found another snag and broke off.

My next attempt was in a larger pool, relatively free of obstructions. I hooked a fish that ran almost to my feet, then turned and dashed upstream—usually a fatal mistake for a steelhead to make, so I began to feel confident of the outcome—but then the hook pulled out.

After this series of defeats it seemed almost anticlimactic when I finally did succeed in landing a steelhead on the midge rod. The fish, a bright six-pounder, took in open water, jumped several times, and put up a good, respectable fight, but in the end it was no match even for the six-foot rod. And although I had the satisfaction of achieving my purpose, there was nothing exceptional about the experience that made me especially want to repeat it; in fact, thinking about it afterwards, it struck me as more of a stunt than a practical method of angling. So after that I retired the six-foot rod from steelhead fishing (although I still use it for trout) and went back to using the eight- and eight-and-a-half-foot rods that I still prefer.

Regardless of its length or the material of its construction, a steelhead fly rod must be matched to the proper type and weight of line. And here, too, there are different schools of thought as to which type of line is best.

As every experienced fly fisher knows, there are basically three types of fly line: The double taper, which is fat in the middle and thin at both ends; the weight-forward taper, which has the thick part at one end while the rest is relatively thin and weightless; and the shooting head, a short length of large-diameter heavy casting line spliced to a long thin length of running line, usually monofilament. The advantage of the double taper is that it allows better control of the line after the cast is made, particularly for mending, but its design makes it more difficult to cast the long distances often required in steelhead fishing. The advantage of the shooting head is that it allows casts of great distance, but the downside is that the angler has almost no control over the line after the cast is made. The weight-forward line is something of a compromise between the other two—it allows fairly long casts and permits at least some degree of control over the line once it is in or on the water, although not nearly as much as a double-tapered line.

My own preference is for the weight-forward design, even for dry-fly work when line control is critically important. But that choice again reflects the habits gained in a lifetime of diverse fly-fishing experience, not just for steelhead; it also is related to the size of the rivers I usually fish, most of which are only of medium size.

The revolution in fly-line development over the past couple of decades has been truly remarkable. The refinement of synthetic materials now used in fly-line manufacture has made it possible to produce lines for almost any specialized angling situation. Thus we now have lines capable of sinking rapidly to the bottom of a deep river even in strong flows, and others with sinking tips of various lengths and specific gravities attached to floating running lines. These and other changes have made it possible for fly anglers to fish effectively in places that were simply beyond their reach not so very long ago.

But not all changes have been for the good. Weight-forward fly lines traditionally have been manufactured in lengths of 35 yards or 105 feet, which is about as much line as a competent caster can reasonably handle, and as much as is needed for most steelhead fly fishing. Some years ago, however, one of the leading line manufacturers quietly cut the length of its weight-forward lines to 27.3 yards, or 82 feet. I knew nothing of this when I bought a new line, checking the label on the box to be certain I had the right type and weight of line but paying no attention to the length, and I didn't notice anything unusual when I loaded the new line on a reel. But the first time I attempted to use it for a long cast across a wide pool—a cast I had made many times before with the thirty-five-yard line I had replaced—I suddenly found I had used up the full length of the new line and was stripping backing off the reel in an effort to get the distance needed. Puzzled, I checked the box and discovered my new line was twenty-three feet shorter than the previous standard. That led me to look in the manufacturer's catalogue, which confirmed that all of his weight-forward lines had been reduced to 27.3 yards.

Not long afterward, the manufacturer's public relations representative wrote to me concerning another matter. In my reply I mentioned my experience and ventured the opinion that his company's weight-forward lines were no longer of sufficient length to satisfy the demands of steelhead fly fishermen. My letter soon came back with a handwritten note from the public relations man scrawled in the margin: "Most people can't cast as far as you can." Perhaps he intended it as a compliment, or maybe even as a joke, but it struck me instead as something of an insult to steelhead fly fishermen, many of whom are much better distance casters than I will ever be. Whatever the public relations man's intent, I have since made it a point to buy all my new lines from another manufacturer that still adheres to the thirty-five-yard standard.

Whatever the choice of rod or line, both must be matched to a good reel. The best reels are works of art in cold metal, solid and strong, heavy and satisfying to the touch, with ever-sparkling polished brightwork. They are machines at rest, just waiting for a strong fish to start them running, and they have a look of action about them even when they are still. And they rank even higher than rods in the affections of many anglers.

These days the tackle magazines are filled with advertisements praising the virtues of a bewildering variety of new reels, and there are more of them all the time. As their numbers have increased, so too have their prices, until now it is possible to pay as much for a single new reel as it cost to buy a dozen good ones not so very many years ago. Unless one opts to fish with the finest handcrafted cane rods, the reel has emerged as the most expensive single item in the modern angler's kit. In fact, reels have become status symbols for those interested in such things, with brand names going in and out of fashion much as they do with luxury automobiles or designer clothing, and the expense of a modern fly reel is often due more to the manufacturer's name and the particular esthetic touches he adds to his product than to any significant increase in functional value.

As with most things, my own disposition is to regard reels more for their utilitarian worth than their status value, although I must admit I am sometimes swayed by esthetic trimmings. And here again I confess a prejudice born from many years of experience with the reels of a single manufacturer. I came of age as an angler at a time when reels made by the British firm of Hardy Bros. were considered as good as any in the world, and the Hardy reels I acquired then—a pair of Zeniths from the famous "Lightweight" series, plus an old St. John—still serve me as faithfully now as they did when I was young, and I have never found any reason to change.

These reels are perfectly suited for my purposes; their capacity for fly line and backing and their adjustable drags are exactly equal to the tasks for which I employ them. In addition to their utilitarian value they have fine esthetic qualities—a simple yet rugged design with clean, satisfying lines and good workmanship. But most satisfying of all is the sound they make when yielding line to a strong fish. Some reels are silent—a great pity—and others emit whispers, rasps, or even high-pitched squeals, but the Hardys have a stern, steady, reassuring sound all their own, a pleasing baritone that somehow seems to convey a sense of the stolid, stiff-upper-lip British manner, if such a thing is possible. To me there is no sweeter sound in angling.

My experience with these reels has been largely trouble-free, although not completely so. The St. John was well used when I bought it from Walt Johnson, who had matched it against the power of many steelhead, and one day while I was fishing the little Green River near Mount St. Helens, the years of wear and tear finally caught up with it. I was stripping line from the reel when the spring holding one of the drag-system pawls broke suddenly and left me with a silent, freespooling reel, lacking either click or drag. Suspecting the cause, I foolishly took the reel apart in midstream; the loose pawl fell out and went to the cobbled bottom in two feet of water.

I realized immediately that this was a potentially serious loss because replacement parts for British reels are very difficult to obtain in North America. So I rolled up my sleeves, got down on my wader-clad knees, plunged my hands into the cold water, and began feeling around in the gravel for the lost pawl. A preliminary search of the area turned up nothing, so I began systematically to pick up each small rock and inspect it, then set it aside. I did this until I had cleared the smaller gravel from several feet of riverbed, leaving nothing but larger rocks, then began using my fingers to probe the narrow crevices between those rocks. Thrusting my right index finger down into one crack, I felt a sudden stabbing pain and quickly drew my hand out; a large, angry crayfish came along with it, its claw clamped firmly around the end of my finger.

That was the last straw, and after I succeeded in prying the crayfish loose from my stinging finger, I gave up the search. Fortunately, I later found a Canadian tackle shop proprietor who had sympathy with my plight and removed a spring and pawl from a new St. John sitting on his shelf and gave them to me, saying he was confident he could get replacement parts. The spring and pawl were quickly installed in my old reel, which has functioned faithfully ever since, and I sincerely hope the proprietor was right about the replacements.

While the Hardys have remained my favorites, other reels have come and gone from my collection over the years. Once I received another British-made reel as a raffle prize; it was a handsome, large-capacity reel, but not as well made as a Hardy, and my experience with it was not nearly as satisfactory. It seized up once while I was playing a large salmon and cost me the fish, and another time the screws that attached it to the reel foot came loose and the reel fell off my rod while I was playing a steelhead. I managed to jam the rod under my left arm and used my left hand to hold the reel while I reeled in awkwardly with my right hand to land the fish, which I was able to do after a long and difficult struggle. Afterward I retired that reel, as I have others that were tried and somehow found wanting.

Rods and reels are the most obvious tools of the steelhead fly fisher's trade, and probably the most loved and sought after, but there are others. Some anglers prize hand-carved wooden wading staffs or handmade leather fly wallets or other custom-crafted objects, and even some mass-produced items have a certain appeal. These include fishing vests, trim and functional, festooned with pockets and ever more becoming part of a fashion state-

ment; metal fly boxes with their long rows of shining empty clips waiting to be filled with the bright works of the tyer's vise, and everything and anything else a steelhead fly fisher needs to carry with him to the stream—waders, wading shoes, stripping baskets, fishing hats, and on and on and on.

Of all these things, the fishing vest is arguably the most important—and potentially the most troublesome. The problem with fishing vests is that some have large pockets, some have many, a few even have both, but nobody yet has succeeded in making a fishing vest with enough pocket space for all the things a steelhead fly fisher wants to carry with him on the river. This is true because of an immutable fact about fishing vests, a sort of Peter Principle of fishing: Stuff expands to exceed pocket capacity. No matter how many pockets in your vest, or how large, inevitably you will find enough indispensable items to fill all of them and then some.

At least that has been true in my case. I would like to be able to use one of the "shorty" fishing vests designed especially for steelheaders who like to wade deep, but their smaller size necessarily means fewer and/or smaller pockets, and that automatically rules them out. Instead I wear a long vest because it offers more pocket capacity, and suffer the routine annoyance of having the lower pockets fill up with water, soaking their contents, whenever I wade deep.

Even the long vest with its greater number of pockets doesn't offer as much carrying capacity as I need. Perhaps I am more of a pack rat than most steelhead fly fishers, but the inventory I carry in my vest doesn't seem unreasonably large: Four reels loaded with different lines, an extra spool carrying a fifth line, two metal fly boxes and a couple of smaller plastic ones, a half-dozen spools of leader material, a small tin of dry-fly dressing, a bottle of sunscreen lotion, two pairs of clippers, and a small hook sharpener. The large pocket in the back of the vest carries a light rain jacket and sometimes a lunch. To me that doesn't seem like very much, but just try to find a vest with pockets enough to hold it all.

There is another inviolable natural law that also has to do with the pockets of fishing vests: No matter how carefully you arrange things in your pockets, they will always rearrange themselves so that the particular item you are looking for is always at the very bottom of the pocket and you will have to remove everything else in order to find it. I don't know how or why this happens, but it is as inevitable as the change of the seasons or the rise and fall of the tide.

Fishing vests have not yet become popular collector's items like rods and reels, but I suppose it will be only a matter of time before they do. Meanwhile, vests serve a vital and necessary functional purpose, and fortunate indeed is the fisherman who finds one that fits properly and comfortably, is not too heavy or too hot, and has almost enough pocket capacity.

Of course it is not necessary to own a great many expensive rods or reels or a deluxe fishing vest in order to be a successful or satisfied steelhead fly fisher. Many anglers do fine with only a single rod, a single reel with an extra spool—one for a floating line, the other for a sinker—and a rudimentary vest with only a few pockets. But tackle collections have a way of starting out small and ending up large, and usually this is due more to the pride and joy of owning interesting and well-made things than to any real necessity. Fine rods and fine reels tend to become objects of affection in the eyes of their owners, things worth having in their own right, and some people even buy them only for display or investment and not for their intended purpose of fishing.

But they are best used for their intended purpose. A rod never flexed under the weight of a heavy steelhead, or a reel never given a chance to sing its excited song to a running fish, are bereft of the memories that make such things really worth having. Such memories—the sight of the rod bowing to a leaping fish, the rising crescendo of the running reel, the wild pounding exhilaration of the angler's heart—become attributes of the things themselves, bound up with them in such a way that you can never again look at them without remembering.

And the value of that is beyond measure.

# 5 | BIG AND LITTLE RIVERS

AT FIRST I wanted to fish them all. I would look at the maps and trace the little blue veins of the rivers with my fingers, then try to figure out how far away they were and whether I had time enough to reach them and give them a fair trial. I would try to remember everything I had heard or read about them and the fishing in them and the size and timing of their steelhead runs.

I did go and fish many of them. I went back to the Wind and the Kalama, since I knew something about each of those rivers from my earlier trips with Ralph Wahl and Enos Bradner, and to the Toutle and its tributary, the cheerful little Green, which I had

explored earlier with Bradner and Joe Pierce, and to many rivers
that were new and unfamiliar: The larger Green River near Seattle, the Skykomish, the Sauk and other Puget Sound rivers, and
the beautiful Sol Duc and Bogachiel, the rushing little Duck-
abush, and the sullen, glacial-colored Hoh on the Olympic Penin-
sula.

Even those days that brought me no fish—and there were still
many of them—yielded profitable experience. I learned more and
more about reading water and judging currents, about diagnosing
likely steelhead lies and approaching them in ways calculated
not to alarm any fish that might be holding in them. I learned
how to take advantage of sunlight or the absence of it, about fly
patterns and their likelihood of success under varying circumstances, and much more about wading.

Each river was a separate experience in itself, and I have always
been fascinated by the way that a river, with the same volume of
water, can be so many different things at once—narrow in some
places and immensely broad in others, swift and roaring here,
slow and sluggish there—and yet always it is the same river. Each
river does the same work, searching ceaselessly for faults in the
rock, feeling always for a new and more comfortable channel,
ever digging, ever burrowing, ever wearing away the texture of the
earth, changing the face of the land even as it draws life into itself
and sustains life along its shores.

Each river also offers unique glimpses of itself—dead leaves
stacked up against rocks in shallow riffles or on the floors of
quiet pools; flotsam hanging in the trees, mute testimony to the
fury of last winter's floods; the hollow husks of hatched-out
stonefly nymphs still clinging to the sun-dried rocks; tiny cork-
screws of current forming randomly in riffles, then disappearing
just as quickly as they formed. Some rivers offer special treats—
the sight of spawning run-of-the-river sockeye salmon decked
out in Christmas-tree colors, the delicate patterns of fresh bird
tracks in soft silt along the river's edge, perhaps the chance to
see an old black bear picking its way carefully across a rock-
slide. Some offer surprises, like the explosive flight of a flock of

mergansers winging swiftly over the water as if shot from a heavy bow.

Sometimes I went with friends but most often I fished alone—except that it is never possible to be completely alone on a river. Everywhere I went I was welcomed by the noisy chatter and darting flight of diving kingfishers; the silent, stately presence of great blue herons; handsome eagles and ospreys wheeling overhead; the awkward antics of dippers at work in the shallows, and all of these became my constant and faithful fishing companions.

Once on the wild upper reaches of the Sauk I waded across the river and stepped out on a sandbar where I looked down and saw the tracks of a large cougar; as I examined them they began to fill with water, which meant the big cat had passed by only seconds before. Nervously I glanced up at the nearby woods, knowing the cougar probably was there watching me, but I saw no sign of it. Encounters with deer were frequent, and once I came upon a pair of large does feeding in an alder copse. Taken by surprise, they froze and let me walk right up to them, close enough to touch, and I stood there and spoke to them softly while they regarded me solemnly with big, curious, liquid brown eyes. Finally they grew tired of my monologue and moved off slowly into the woods, glancing back over their shoulders now and then to see if I was still watching until finally they were swallowed up in the heavy timber. They left deep tracks in the soft earth and I wondered if time would freeze them there forever, like dinosaur tracks in the ancient stone of Texas.

All these and countless other little things I saw and sensed and felt while fishing, and all of them helped me to understand how and why rivers are as powerful in their attraction for men as they are for steelhead and salmon. With all this to enjoy, the fact that one also might have a chance to take a steelhead on the fly seemed like an unreasonable bonus, much more than one should sensibly expect as his fair share of the wonders a river has to offer. But some days brought that reward, too—or, if not a fish on the beach, then at least a momentary connection with one.

One day on the Holy Water of the Kalama I walked out onto a

thrusting point of ledge rock, looked down into the deep slot of river that skirted the edge of it, and saw the gray backs of a pair of summer steelhead lying almost underfoot. There was no way to reach them from above, so I stayed where I was and cast directly upstream, letting the current carry the sinking fly back down to the fish. The water was deep but clear enough that I could see the fly coming, turning over and over in the current as it swept downstream. Then one of the fish saw it too, moved to meet it, and took the fly right before my eyes. I waited a moment for the current to carry the line past the fish, then recovered slack and struck hard.

The steelhead bolted out of the slot and into the quiet water of an upstream pool, then jumped high, throwing spats of silver spray. It fell back and burrowed into the depths of the pool until suddenly its throbbing life was replaced by a sullen dead weight, and my heart sank as I realized the fish had found a snag. I pulled as hard as I dared, but the leader would not break and I feared the line itself was caught. Rather than risk breaking it, I waded out into the pool, inching deeper and deeper until wavelets were lapping around my wader tops as I followed the taut line toward whatever held it fast. At last I found the snag, an old submerged limb with the line wrapped tightly in a double turn around it, and feeling awkwardly under water with fumbling fingers I finally managed to free it. It was no surprise to find both the fly and the fish were missing from the end of the leader, but at least I had gotten the fly line back—and I will always remember the sight of that fish taking the fly right before my eyes.

Another time on the Holy Water I hiked down through the brush to a favorite pool just in time to see another angler wade out in front of me. I felt the familiar frustration that a fisherman always feels when he sees that someone else has beaten him to the best water, but there was no help for it, so I went upstream to try a less-productive stretch while I waited for the other fisherman to fish through the pool, hoping he would leave any steelhead that might be waiting there.

I kept an eye on him as I fished the upper water and soon noticed he was using a fly rod with what appeared to be a gigantic automatic reel attached. He was fishing leisurely and taking his time, which made me all the more impatient, and he hadn't covered more than half the pool when a good steelhead took him. The fish leaped once and started off on a long downstream run; farther and farther it ran, winding the spring in the big automatic reel tighter and tighter, and I could sense what was going to happen next: The fisherman accidentally brushed a finger against the reel's automatic-retrieve lever and even from where I was, far upstream, I could hear the pop of his leader breaking. The line came flying back in his face, and for a selfish moment I felt perversely glad. Had I been first into the pool I might have hooked that fish, so it somehow seemed right to me that the other fisherman had lost it in such an ignominious fashion. But when my turn came to fish the pool I could not raise another fish, and perhaps it served me right for thinking such ill thoughts toward another fisherman.

I fished most often in summer and fall, when the stream flows were stable and temperatures were comfortable, but sometimes I also went out on winter days when the rivers were low and clear enough to fish with a fly. Always there was more competition in the winter months, most of it from anglers who fished with bait or lures and seemed unwilling to respect the distance a fly fisherman needs to have around him, and sometimes it was necessary to search long and hard for an unoccupied stretch of river.

Even so, searching for a place to fish usually was the easiest part of a day of winter steelheading. The cruel cold of the water and the air imposed handicaps unknown in summer fishing, especially for a fly fisherman who must always use his hands to cast and control the line. Cold slows everything down, fish as well as fishermen—but only until a fish is hooked, and then it may respond as quickly and wildly as a summer steelhead in warm water. That gives the fish an advantage, for even the flow of adrenalin that fills an angler's veins when a heavy steelhead takes his fly often is not enough to overcome the sluggishness imposed by relentless cold.

Another difference is the absence of color in winter. In the summer and fall there is color everywhere; in the winter there is only black and white and shades of gray. The rivers are gray, the skies are gray, the barren trees along the riverbanks are skeletal and black, and the frozen fields beyond them are covered with white patches of old decaying snow, like spots of fungus.

Winter also is a quiet time. There is no foliage to fling back the sounds of the river, so it seems hushed and quiet even when there is no fresh snow to help absorb the sound. The songs of summer birds are distant memories and the woods and fields are silent except for the sporadic hoarse cries of ravens. The ice-rimmed edges of the quiet pools hold the half-decayed carcasses of the last spawned-out salmon, and these ever-present reminders of death seem somehow in keeping with the mood and pace of the season. Yet even in the cold, slow, swollen winter rivers the fish are there. They come to the fly with a long, deliberate pull, if they come at all, and once hooked they turn away quickly and run or jump with heavy, ponderous strength.

One January day I went up to a long pool on the North Fork of the Stillaguamish, a pool that always seemed too low in summer to hold fish but looked as if it might hold them during the heavier winter flow. A thick wet snow was falling by the time I got there, the kind of snow that melts and soaks you when it hits, and soon the heavy wet flakes closed in around me and hid the far bank of the river and everything else except for a dull gray patch of water directly in my front. The river had risen until it was level with the grassy bank so that I was into it with only a single step, and the shock of its cold water came instantly through my waders. With wet fingers threatening quickly to grow numb, I tied on a big bright fly dressed on a heavy nickel-plated hook and began fishing. Snowflakes ebbed and flowed around me, parting now and then just long enough to afford a brief glimpse of dark alders on the far shore, then closing in again.

I fished through the head of the run, then hung my fly on an underwater snag and had to break it off. I went ashore to change flies, stamping my feet and rubbing my hands to try to bring back a little circulation and warmth, then returned to the river for another try.

I suppose I had fished the better part of an hour before the fish took. It intercepted the fly early in its drift and at first my fingers were too numb to detect the gradual tightening of the line. But then the line was pulled strongly from my grasp and there was no longer any doubt; the fish ran upstream, porpoised once, then turned and headed down toward a spot where I could see the tips of submerged limbs dancing in the current. I reared back on the rod, reeled hard, and swung the fish around, back out into the main flow. It stayed there a while, deep down and out of sight, and I could feel long, slow movements coming back through the line while the fish shook its head from side to side.

It was not a spectacular fish, but it was strong and stood its ground stubbornly and we slugged it out together in the silent, swirling snow. After what seemed a long time its strength began to ebb and it came in grudgingly, contesting every inch of line, until at last I could see its vague silver shape in the gray water lapping up against the overhanging grass. Finally I brought it close enough that I could reach down, grasp the big fly stuck firmly in the side of its jaw, and twist it free. At first the fish did not realize it was free; it lay still for a long moment so that I was able to get a good look at it and see that it was a buck steelhead of about nine pounds with a hefty kype on the tip of its lower jaw. Then it came to life and swam wearily out of sight, leaving me alone and shivering—partly from the effort and partly from the chill.

I remember another winter day when I made my way to the Skykomish, which then was much less crowded and offered much easier access than is the case now. There had been bitter weather for a week and everything was frozen; the pasture grass crackled and bent like thin wire as I walked through it on my way to the river, and when I came out on a long gravel bar I could see that all the rocks were rimmed with ice like bricks set in silvery mortar. The icy air made the skin of my face feel stiff and stretched, and the river, when I entered it, was so cold it was painful to my legs and feet even inside the heavy waders. A pale sun floated distantly overhead in the hazy blue sky, and the foothills all around were bright with new-fallen snow.

I started fishing at the head of a long run with moderate depth and flow, throwing a big fly on a long sinking line and mending the line quickly to hold the fly in the current and give it a chance to sink well down. In this manner I worked my way slowly downstream, wiggling my toes every now and then to try to keep some semblance of warmth and feeling in my lower limbs. It was cruel, hard fishing, the cold robbing me of the pleasure of it, and as I

came to the end of the run I found myself wondering if there were
any purpose in it.

That thought was quickly stilled by a sudden savage strike.
The force of it surprised me—it was not like the usual deliberate
take of a winter steelhead—and the fish reacted more swiftly
than I did; it ran immediately, tearing yards of backing from the
reel. The run stopped as quickly as it started, with the fish somewhere down in a patch of shallow choppy water well below. I
followed along the bank, reeling all the while, until I came to a
place where the bank fell away sharply into deep water and the
way around was blocked by a thick stand of barren cottonwoods.
Unable to go farther, I knew I would have to settle the issue
where I was. The fish was still on, somewhere far out in the river,

but try as I might I couldn't move it. There was something odd about the way it was fighting; its movements now seemed sluggish and heavy and it didn't run again, or jump. It simply resisted, and I struggled to recover line, turn by stubborn turn.

After a long, sullen battle that resembled a tug-of-war more than anything else, I managed to wrench the fish up close enough to discover the reason for its odd behavior: It was hooked squarely through the tail. Apparently it had made a pass at my fly and missed, then hooked itself as it turned away. It protested vigorously as I led it backward to the ice-rimmed rocks along the river's edge, then thrashed about until I could pin it down with one hand long enough to remove the fly with the other. I held it upright in the icy river until its strength returned—along with perhaps a little of its dignity—and it was able to make its way slowly back out into the cold, clear flow of the main current.

On most of my weekend fishing trips I stayed in steelhead towns. These may be a phenomenon peculiar to the Pacific Northwest, sleepy little places that fate has chanced to plunk down near some important river. In most cases they started life as logging communities, and logging is still the mainstay of existence for many of them, but over the years they also have become important to fishermen—places like Forks, Castle Rock and Darrington, little neon oases in the cut-over woods where anglers can go to spend the nights before or after fishing. A fisherman usually sees them in the darkness or in the half light of the dawn, frequently under rain, and they do not present their best faces then.

Each steelhead town has at least one motel that caters mostly to fishermen, and these establishments are all pretty much the same. Most appear to have been built about the time automatic transmissions were invented, and typically one or more of the neon letters will have burned out of the sign that announces their shabby existence. Beneath the main sign is usually another one that simply says NO, the owners having decided it was unnecessary to also invest in the word VACANCY. Their offices display brochures and business cards of local steelhead guides on

the counter next to a hand bell that is used to summon the owner
from his television set in the back room. Often there is a
mounted steelhead on the wall, a long-dead fish now frozen perpetually in a taxidermic leap, its colors dulled by generations of
cigarette smoke. Sometimes the fins show vivid scars where they
were glued back in place after a fall from the trophy's lofty perch.

The motel rooms smell of old cigars and stale beer and the
beds are lumpy and damp. The end tables have milky overlapping
rings left by condensation from glasses filled with ice and whiskey, the wallpaper curls like cedar bark, and although the television set is bolted down, the switch still comes off in your hand
when you try to change channels. It matters little; there is heavy
snow on some channels, light snow on the others. The toilet runs
and sounds like the river you are going to fish tomorrow until
you get up and jiggle the handle. The drawers hold a Gideon Bible

and a few postcards showing how the motel looked when it was new, three or four owners ago.

Each steelhead town also has at least one restaurant that begins its day very early because that is when loggers and steelhead fishermen begin theirs. Its potholed parking lot is filled with logging trucks and four-wheel-drive rigs hitched to trailers bearing river boats or jet sleds, and inside the place is warm and smells of cigarette smoke, coffee and grease, and it is always noisy with conversation and the clatter of cups and dishes. The waitresses, whose main job is to keep every coffee cup full, go about their work with bland, bored looks on their faces; they are not looking forward to their day nearly as much as you are looking forward to yours.

Some Northwest rivers have steelhead lodges that are famous for their comfort and cuisine, and a few fishermen are lucky enough to stay in such places. But many of them—the great cadre of hardcore working steelhead fishermen, the blue-collar, cigar-smoking, whiskey-drinking, poker-playing weekend fishermen—stay in these run-down, out-of-the-way little towns that are only specks on the highway maps. During my early days as a steelhead fisherman, I often stayed in them too.

But I always much preferred to camp along rivers whenever it was possible to do so. Along the rivers the evening air was always fresh and clean and cool, the campfires always warm and welcome, and the soothing sound of rushing water—sometimes mixed with the drumming of rain on tent or camper roof—always helped sleep come easily. In summer months the songbirds never failed to give an early wake-up call, and I soon learned that a crackling morning fire and the scent of fresh coffee brewing near a riverbank are among the greatest of life's simple pleasures.

During those early years I fished many rivers I have never since revisited and others to which I have returned time and time again. I suppose it was natural that after a while some of the latter began to assume the status of special favorites and I began going back to them more and more often.

One of these was the little Green River, which spilled happily down from the logging-scarred foothills of Mount St. Helens. The Green had a fine summer run of big steelhead, some so large they seemed out of scale for such a small river, and often they were visible and highly vulnerable in the clear water of the river's diminutive pools and runs. Of course they knew this and were always wary and easily spooked, and so I learned more from them than I did from the steelhead of any other river—more about the need for careful stalking and a quiet approach, more about the type of water the fish preferred at various levels of the river, and much more about the many subtleties and nuances of steelhead fly fishing at close quarters—things frequently unnecessary or forgotten on larger rivers.

At the lower end of the Green was a salmon hatchery that provided easy access to the stream, and the water above and below the hatchery had been declared a fly-fishing-only area. The river there was small enough to wade easily, though its gravel was always slick and the footing never certain, and most of its pools could be covered with a roll cast. And despite its ever-wary and nervous steelhead and the ever-present need for caution, the Green always was a generous river—perhaps the most generous steelhead river I have ever fished.

My first visit to the river one year was early in July with Ralph Wahl, Ted Rogowski and Ray Kotrla. My diary entry for that day briefly noted the changes wrought by winter floods, but most of the entry was devoted to the remarkable fishing:

". . . I went down to the split in the river where formerly there had been a big logjam. Now there is a long, smooth run with fair depth and good flow. I had fished more than halfway down when I had a terrific take and a great fish leaped twice toward the foot of the pool—a fine, bright steelhead of about ten pounds. I was afraid it would head down through the rapids, but it turned and ran hard the full length of the pool and jumped again, a high twisting leap, and fell back with a loud crash. Then the fish ran into the remaining logs and broke me. The experience left me shaken . . .

"Afterward I fished the last pool (above the confluence with the Toutle) without success, then hiked back nearly to the hatchery. Ralph had brought down some sandwich fixings, so we ate on the river and resumed fishing. I fished again as far as the last pool without success. But then in the last pool I had a good strike on about my tenth cast. The fish did not fight particularly well—one jump and one good run—and in five minutes I had it on the beach, a handsome buck of six or seven pounds . . . After a few more casts I left the pool to Rogowski and went up to the next pool. Again I hooked a fish right away, but quickly lost it. And that it was it for the day. But what a good one it was—three steelhead hooked and one landed. Ralph also hooked and lost a fish, and so did Ted. Lots of fish in the river."

Two weeks later I returned and made this entry in my diary: "Saw fish in virtually every pool but had no takers until I reached the second pool above the Toutle. The situation and time of day were nearly identical to two weeks ago—the tail of the pool was in shadow and it was about 4 P.M. I cast in nearly the same place and a steelhead took just as I began to retrieve. It jumped once and then to my dismay it ran out of the pool and down into the rapids below. I followed it down, but it ran the line around a rock. I waded out and freed the line and found the fish was still on. It ran across the stream and took the leader around a limb and I had to wade across through the fast water to free it—something I never could have done in the higher water two weeks ago.

"To my surprise when the line was clear the fish was still on and I managed to lead it away from the brush. It ran downstream out of the rapids into quiet water, and then I knew I had it. After a couple more short rushes I eased it up on the sand—a fine, bright buck of seven or eight pounds with my No. 6 Skunk stuck firmly in its lower jaw. It also had a No. 10 bait hook stuck in its gullet and about eight inches of leader trailing out through its gill . . ."

The Green was my undoubted favorite for several seasons and I felt the loss very keenly when it was struck savagely by the great shock wave from the 1980 explosion of Mount St. Helens, which left it choked with ash, mud, and fallen timber; it was something like experiencing the death of an old friend. But I'm certain the sense of loss would have been much greater if by then, in the fickle way of fishermen, I had not switched my affections to a different river.

This was the North Fork of the Stillaguamish and my interest in it, always more than passing, had been greatly enhanced by the fact that I had purchased Enos Bradner's old fishing cabin just below the river's junction with Deer Creek, the principal summer steelhead spawning tributary in the Stillaguamish system. Ownership of the cabin meant for the first time that I had ready access to some of the very best water on the North Fork, and it had the added advantage of being much closer to home than the little Green.

So the North Fork was about to become my home river. After spending the better part of a decade rushing around the Pacific Northwest trying to fish nearly every steelhead river within reach, I now faced the prospect of settling down and devoting my full attention to only a single river—or at least to one above all others. And in years to come the majority of my steelhead fly-fishing adventures would be played out on the familiar, friendly waters of the North Fork.

# 6 | THE ART OF WADING

MORE THAN twenty years have passed since the last time I
fell into a river. To be sure, there have been some close calls since
then, and a few times when I have shipped water over the tops of
my waders while chasing a running fish or trying to negotiate a
heavy stretch of deep water, but those incidents were intentional,
so they don't count. Neither do all the times my waders leaked,
because that almost seems to be a natural condition of waders.
Having said all that, I suppose now I shall go out on the river
tomorrow and take a big spill.

But I doubt it—because I have two things going for me now

that I lacked twenty years ago. One is confidence, the feeling that I can handle almost anything a river can throw at me. The other is experience, which helps me to recognize when the river is gaining the upper hand so I can exercise the discretion to withdraw. When it comes to wading wild steelhead rivers, discretion is certainly the better part of valor, and it helps to have the experience to be able to tell when it's time to forget valor and begin thinking about discretion.

The ability to wade well is a vital part of steelhead fly fishing,

an acquired skill as critical to success as the ability to cast a fly. Wading also is a skill that offers its own unique rewards, and for me it has become one of the greatest pleasures of steelhead fly fishing.

But I suspect that may not be true for all anglers. For every bold wader who enjoys the challenge of heavy water, it seems there is a timid one who shies away from it. These usually are fishermen who never have learned proper wading techniques or developed the confidence that comes from such knowledge, and for them wading remains a necessary evil—something to be endured rather than enjoyed.

Of course, all anglers start out timidly. That's not surprising; if you are unaccustomed to it, the experience of entering a wild steelhead river can be pretty intimidating: There is the swift, cold, often deep current to contend with, the icy slipperiness of unsteady boulders underfoot, the frightening roar of white water close at hand. It's enough to make you wonder what you are doing there and whether this is all worthwhile. Some fishermen resolve that question in the negative, and perhaps that is yet another way the process of natural selection thins the ranks of potential steelhead fly fishers.

Those who do stick with it tread cautiously and tentatively at first, carefully avoiding all water that appears remotely fraught with hazard—even though such water often holds the greatest promise of fish. But despite all such cautious measures a fall at some point is inevitable, and when it comes it happens in the merest fraction of an instant: Suddenly your balance is lost, the river has you in its clutches, you feel the shock of its cold water filling your waders and coming through your shirt, and it sucks your breath away. The current carries you along and you wonder wildly where it will take you and what it will do with you when it gets there, and you have a mighty urge to struggle and resist.

All of this is psychological, of course; this is the same river you might willingly enter on a hot day while wearing a swimsuit and enjoy yourself mightily; the only difference is that this time you are wearing waders and a fishing vest and you hadn't planned to get wet. But if you relax and keep your wits about you, things will usually turn out well. True, you may emerge sputtering, wet, miserable, and feeling as if the river had washed away the last shred of your dignity, but you can take comfort from the knowledge that virtually every fisherman has had the same humbling experience at one time or another. Falling into a river is simply a rite of passage, an informal baptism required for admission into the religious order of steelhead fly fishing.

I write from experience. That fall twenty-plus years ago took place on the North Fork of the Skykomish, where I had gone alone to search for summer steelhead. I was wearing a pair of boot-foot waders with felt soles, and because I was still learning about wading and lacking in confidence, I waded out very slowly and tentatively as far as I dared go into a waist-deep run that tumbled down into a wide, handsome pool. Each unsteady rock of the cobbled bottom was coated with a thin film of grease-slick algae and the felt soles of my waders seemed to offer little traction on the slippery rock surfaces, a fact that did little for my already shaky confidence. Cautiously I edged outward until I was thigh-deep in the flow, which turned out to be even stronger than it looked.

Having gone as far as I thought I could safely go, I began to fish, throwing a wet fly on a moderately long line across the run and fishing it downstream. After each couple of casts I shuffled down a step or two, closer to the big pool at the foot of the run. I hadn't made very many casts before I was suddenly aware that my feet were no longer in contact with the bottom. The river had lifted me gently and was carrying me downstream toward the center of the pool, and in an instant I was beyond any bottom I could touch. Then water was pouring in over the tops of my waders and soaking through my fishing vest and shirt and I felt the icy shock of it at the same moment I felt an icy pang of fear. Involuntarily, I reached up and grabbed my hat with one hand while I held onto my fly rod with the other and tried to swallow the panic I could feel rising in my throat.

The feeling of panic lasted only a moment and it was then that I actually began to enjoy what was happening. It was a hot day and I had been warm; the sudden coolness of the river felt good. The sky overhead was a soft summer blue and the moss-covered boulders and deep green firs along the river's edge made a pleasing contrast as I glided effortlessly past them. I seemed to be in no danger of sinking and it was no problem keeping my head above water; I decided to relax and see where the river would take me.

It took me nearly a hundred yards downstream, all the way through the broad pool—much deeper than I was tall—and deposited me gently on a gravel bar near the tail-out. My feet struck the gravel and planted firmly, the current lifted me gently upright, and the ride was over as suddenly as it had begun. It almost seemed as if the river had enjoyed a little joke at my expense.

I went ashore, took off my waders, and dumped out a couple of quarts of water, wrung out my socks and shirt, put everything back on, and fished through the rest of the day in pleasantly damp coolness.

So it all turned out well. But the experience taught me that I had much to learn about wading and made me determined to learn what I needed to know. For that purpose I turned to books, as I have so often for the answers to questions about fly fishing, and as usual I was not disappointed—for although I did not find a great deal of written advice on the subject of wading, what I did find was sound and more than adequate. And I quickly began practicing the techniques described in the books.

For the most part these were simple and basic. Boiled down, they really amounted to a couple of fundamental rules: Always keep your body parallel to the flow so it offers less resistance to the current, and take only a single step at a time, planting one foot firmly before you move the other one. These were things I already had been doing intuitively, but it helped to know they were the right things and to practice them deliberately. And though they seemed simple enough, it was surprising at first how often I forgot about them when I got into difficult circumstances, and I probably would have suffered additional dunkings if I hadn't remembered a couple of other techniques my reading had disclosed.

One was that if you get into trouble, it's best to stop, take a deep breath, relax, and try to analyze the situation carefully. If you've waded into a tough spot where the only escape is to turn around and go back the way you came, then you should always turn upstream, into the current, never away from it. In such situations it's also important to keep your feet relatively close together; don't let them get straddled on either side of a boulder. And if you start to lose your balance, throw out your arms; that may help you regain it. If you actually start to fall, thrust your fly rod full-length into the water in front of you; the water resistance against the rod will give you a moment's leverage that may be just enough to let you recover your balance.

That last maneuver sounds unlikely, but the first time I tried it I found out that it worked—much to my surprise and relief—and it has since kept me dry on a number of occasions.

Some things I learned from experience. Perhaps the most important was the need to maintain concentration at all times; that first unwary step after your attention has been diverted is often the one that will get you into trouble. Another was more a matter of attitude than technique, a sort of mental determination never to yield the initiative to the river—because, from a psychological standpoint, once you let the river gain the upper hand you're almost certainly headed for a dunking. And naturally the more I waded, the more practical knowledge I gained about the kinds of water that can be waded safely, and the kinds to avoid.

With all this I began to find growing pleasure in wading—a feeling of satisfaction at having successfully negotiated a difficult stretch of water, or the equally satisfying knowledge at the end of a long day that I had both fished and waded well. These added to the rewards of fishing, coming as a sort of unexpected bonus that helped to fill the cup of memories, especially on fishless days.

I also learned when it was wise not to wade. The whole object of wading is to place oneself in the most favorable position for fishing, and since that is the object, one of the most important fundamentals is to know when it is necessary to wade and when to hold back. Countless times I have seen anglers wade into the water they should have been fishing and begin fishing the water they should have been wading—if, indeed, they should have been wading at all.

Sometimes it is best to stay out of the water altogether; many fine stretches of steelhead water can be covered more effectively by casting from the bank, and if there is no need to risk disturbing fish by wading when one should not wade. Steelhead also sometimes move into the shallows near the riverbanks when the water is cloudy or during the twilight of early morning or late evening, and unnecessary wading at such times can easily spook them and send them flying in panic. The best advice is to be conservative and wade only when it is absolutely necessary. And when it is necessary, then one should always wade quietly and deliberately and try to avoid creating ripples that may disturb the surface of a quiet pool.

As I gained more and more wading experience I also developed more and more confidence. Confidence is a wonderful feeling; it makes you believe you can do almost anything. But confidence in wading ability can be a two-edged sword; one can become *too* confident and begin to take unnecessary risks. It would not do to make light of the potential seriousness of these risks; many steelhead rivers are big, violent, and enormously strong; wading them is tricky under the best of circumstances, and there is never a guarantee that things are going to turn out well if you should slip and fall. Sometimes they don't turn out well; the Dean River in British Columbia has claimed the lives of at least two wading fishermen that I know of, and just last year the gentle North Fork of the Stillaguamish, even at its lowest summer flow, took the life of a fisherman who slipped and fell while wading.

I was once a witness to such a tragedy and will never forget it. It happened on the Waikato River in New Zealand, a big stream that resembles a typical Northwest steelhead river in many respects. A fisherman wading in the river not far below its source in Lake Taupo was swept away by the swift current and carried downstream into the maelstrom of Huka Falls, where the whole broad width of the Waikato squeezes itself into a narrow rocky passage and rushes downhill with incredible force into a vast lake-sized pool. I came upon the scene moments later and joined the growing crowd of people frantically searching the pool below the falls for a sign of the fisherman while a rescue helicopter hovered overhead.

Suddenly a shout went up as we caught sight of something bobbing in the current near one of the steep cliffs bordering the edge of the pool. The helicopter pilot saw it too, and in a daring piece of flying he maneuvered his machine so close to the cliff that the helicopter's rotor blades began chopping bits of foliage from shrubs clinging to the rock wall. Ignoring the danger, he held the craft steady while another crew member lowered a grappling hook, snagged the object in the current, and hoisted it up so that we could all see what it was: An empty pair of waders.

It was several more days before the body of the unfortunate angler was found and recovered, well downstream from Huka Falls. But I'll never forget the sight of those empty waders being hoisted from the stormy waters of the Waikato, or the sick feeling it gave me in the pit of my stomach, and the recollection of that tragic incident will forever keep me from growing too confident of my ability to master difficult waters. No fisherman should ever underestimate the risks of wading steelhead rivers, especially if he is a visitor to the Northwest without prior knowledge of its streams.

Proper conditioning helps reduce the risk. Wading all day in heavy, cold currents over slippery bottoms requires a full measure of strength, agility, and endurance, and a good wader necessarily should also be a good athlete. Leg strength is particularly important, and at least some training is necessary to keep one's legs in shape for wading.

As a younger man I played basketball year-round to keep my legs strong for wading, but then I suffered an injury that crippled my casting arm for more than six months and ended my days on the basketball court. Now I do a lot of walking to keep my legs in shape, and Seattle's steep hills are well suited for the purpose. It also helps to have a physical build like mine, which has been described as similar to that of a cedar stump; it takes a lot of current to move someone built like I am.

Safe wading also requires the right equipment. There may be occasions during the warm weather and low water of late summer when it is more comfortable to wade wet than to wear boots or waders, but at all other times waders are desirable if not absolutely necessary. And these should always be chest waders; hip boots are inadequate for any but the smallest steelhead streams.

It seems that a civilization capable of producing pressurized suits that enable men to walk safely on the airless surface of the moon should also be capable of manufacturing chest waders that do not leak on their first immersion, but unfortunately that often seems not to be the case. Things have gotten better in recent years, but it's still possible to spend a lot of money for a deluxe pair of waders and have them leak the first time they are used. Even if they don't leak the first time, they may not last long enough to warrant the cost.

My solution to this problem has been to buy inexpensive waders, usually priced at only a sixth to a quarter of the cost of top-of-the-line models. If these inexpensive waders leak, then I'm not out very much money—and usually they last for at least a season or two, after which I can throw them away and buy another pair of the same kind. I doubt I would get much additional wear from a more expensive pair of waders, assuming they were any good to begin with, so over time I believe I am money ahead.

Not that this approach doesn't involve some compromises. The inexpensive waders I buy usually are made of lightweight material and lack insulation of any kind. This can make them rather uncomfortable for winter fishing, and even the heaviest long underwear and wool socks aren't quite enough to mitigate the chill of a cold winter river. So the reality is that if you wear waders of this kind for winter fishing you can't stay in the water as long as you could with a heavier pair of insulated waders. The thin material also makes inexpensive waders especially vulnerable to puncture wounds from hidden strands of barbed wire or blackberry vines, so you must always be watchful while walking to or from the river.

The synthetic materials used in the manufacture of most inexpensive waders also have a tendency to deteriorate over time, especially if exposed to sunlight, so when you buy a pair it's always a good idea to find out how long they've been on the shelf in the store—and whether the shelf is in front of a window. As the late angling writer Harmon Henkin so aptly put it, waders, like doughnuts, should always be purchased fresh.

In my early days of steelhead fishing I preferred boot-foot waders, which have a built-in shoe or boot and require nothing more in the way of footgear, but it was not very long before I discarded them as being too heavy and awkward. Now I use only stocking-foot waders that fit comfortably into separate laced-up wading shoes; this combination makes a lightweight outfit that allows maximum freedom of movement. Good-quality wading shoes are essential, but like waders most wading shoes are badly overpriced. After shopping around I found a sturdy pair for under forty dollars; they are now in their third season and still just like new. Gravel guards worn over the tops of the wading shoes add comfort and protection and may extend the life of both shoes and waders.

Perhaps the biggest question in terms of wading equipment is what to wear on the soles of boot-foot waders or wading shoes. Felt is considered a sort of universal traction-giving substance, but even good felt may not provide enough traction for safe footing on the algae-slickened boulders and bedrock ledges of most lowland Northwest steelhead rivers. Felt also is susceptible to rapid wear and damage; I ruined two sets of felts in just four days of wading over the razor-sharp shale found in many parts of Oregon's Deschutes River. The sharp rock edges simply cut the felt to pieces.

Outdoor carpeting is another alternative, and if it is of good quality it will wear better than felt and offer almost equal traction. But no matter how carefully you follow the instructions for gluing it on, it never stays put—or at least it never has for me.

Some years ago a fishing companion gave me a pair of Korkers and I thought then that I had found the ultimate in wading footgear. Korkers are hard-rubber strap-on sandals with metal calks protruding from their soles, long used by Northwest loggers and longshoremen for working on wet docks and other slippery surfaces. Gradually they were also adopted for use by steelhead fishermen, who discovered their metal calks cut through algae and slime and gave excellent traction—far superior to felt—on even the most treacherous rocks. My own wading competence and confidence both quickly increased when I tried the pair my friend had given me. I wore that pair until it was in tatters, then bought another pair and another after that.

But even Korkers are not without problems. No matter how tightly you strap them on, they have a disconcerting habit of coming off when you're wading through soft mud or silt. The steel calks also wear down quickly and are difficult to replace, requiring special tools and a great deal of patience. Calks made from tungsten steel are available and these last somewhat longer, but they are surprisingly expensive, and even they wear out in time.

Not that it matters, for I have since found something I like even better than Korkers. These are stream cleats, rubber overshoes designed to fit tightly over wading shoes, with felt soles and metal cleats on the bottom. The overshoes can be put on or taken off much more easily and quickly than Korkers and they don't come off in mud or silt. The thick metal cleats do eventually wear out, but they last much longer than the metal calks on Korkers, and, if anything, give even better traction. Their only drawback is that they make a lot of noise, but that can be minimized by careful wading. In my view they are the ultimate traction device for steelhead fly fishers.

To this point I have not mentioned wading staffs. These are a matter of contention with some anglers, who regard their use as a sign of weakness or an acknowledgement that an angler has reached an age where his legs are uncertain and in danger of failing. I do not share this view. In my opinion wading staffs are highly useful pieces of equipment in situations where they are needed; they can give an angler a "third leg" that will help him keep his footing in the most difficult water. But they can also get in the way and be an annoyance, and they can be noisy, and for those reasons I use one only when I have to.

The lower Wenatchee River is one place where I feel more comfortable with a wading staff than without one. It is a river with a deceptively strong current, a great number of rocks about the size and smoothness of bowling balls, and a healthy growth of algae that covers everything below the surface with a slippery coat of what might just as well be grease. That combination makes the Wenatchee as difficult to wade as any river I have ever fished, and on those occasions when I have fished it without a wading staff I have come perilously close to taking some unscheduled baths.

So far the Wenatchee is the only river where I feel the need to use a wading staff, but as age continues to take its toll on the joints and muscles of my legs I suspect there will be more such rivers. However, I have no false sense of pride that will keep me from using a wading staff wherever and whenever I think it is necessary.

With experience, confidence, and the proper equipment, there is no reason a modern steelhead fly fisher should not feel comfortable in the great majority of wading situations, even including turbid waters where the bottom is invisible, or in wading at night if he knows the water well enough. Yet despite all this—or perhaps partly because of it—the value of good wading skills seems in danger of becoming lost, or at least downgraded. With such devices as stream cleats and wading staffs and the ability to cast farther with new high-technology rods and lines, the need for good wading skills has diminished and more and more anglers have neglected this part of their education.

Heavy fishing pressure is another contributing factor. These days, with a steady procession of anglers moving through the most popular pools hour after hour and day after day, there has become a sort of mindless tendency for fishermen to follow the guy in front of them and wade where he wades. As a result, many of the same fishermen who have neglected their wading skills also have largely forfeited the use of any imagination in wading— and hence also in their fishing.

The bad news about all this is that wading may become a lost art. The good news is that those who have been at the business long enough to have learned their wading lessons well may now use that knowledge to advantage over other fishermen. By that I mean that in today's heavily fished steelhead streams, the angler who knows how to wade where others fear to tread may have a better chance of success.

This observation is based on the assumption that if a steelhead spends its whole day watching a parade of flies come into view from exactly the same angle and swing overhead in exactly the same fashion, it's not likely to pay attention to them very long; but if suddenly it sees one coming from a wholly different direction and behaving in a wholly different manner, it might well be tempted to respond. In other words, if you see other fishermen following in one another's footsteps, wading and fishing a pool in exactly the same fashion, then it might pay dividends to wade out farther, or try to fish the pool from an entirely different angle, or perhaps even to cross the river and fish it from the opposite shore. At least that is my theory, and although I can't yet say there is enough evidence to support its absolute validity, I have often used a different wading approach to take fish after a whole succession of other anglers had fished the same drift unsuccessfully.

The famous Deer Creek Riffle on the North Fork of the Stillaguamish is a case in point. There may not be another piece of steelhead water in all creation that gets pounded as heavily as the Deer Creek Riffle, with a steady picket fence of anglers moving through it day after day from before dawn until well after dusk. Virtually every angler fishes it the same way, entering the head of

the run from the north side and stepping downstream after every few casts (at least the courteous ones do) until they have covered all the most productive water, after which they may get back in line and fish through the pool again in exactly the same manner, changing only the pattern of their flies.

Having taken my own place in this endless rotation on a number of occasions, I have often been struck by the monotony of it; it's a wonder the steelhead don't die of sheer boredom. To break up the sameness of this approach, I have several times waded across the river to the south bank and fished the riffle from there. At high water the crossing is not an easy one, and over-hanging brush on the south side mandates the use of roll casts, and these obstacles seem to discourage other anglers from trying the same thing—assuming they have ever conceived the idea. But more than once this approach has brought me a quick hook-up with a steelhead after the endless shuffling procession of anglers on the far bank had cast to the same water for hours on end without result.

So I believe that on heavily fished streams it pays to watch how others fish and then adopt a different approach, and good wading skills are essential for this strategy. Of course there are also risks involved; if you wade out farther than anyone else, you may find yourself wading in among the fish—and then nobody will be able to catch them. Like anything else in steelhead fly fishing, prudence should be your guide.

But on those days when everything works well—when the wading and the fishing are good, when you use all your skill and wit to overcome the perpetual force of the river, to navigate suc-cessfully over slippery stones and through tricky currents to a point beyond the reach of other anglers, when a good fish takes and the results are everything you could possibly desire—then you will experience the full pleasure and satisfaction that comes from knowing the art of wading. For doubt not that wading *is* an art.

# 7 | HOME RIVER

THE WADERS hang from the cabin rafters, drying slowly in the warmth of a whispering fire. The fly rods are suspended on nails driven at equal intervals into the cabin walls, and the fishing vests hang limply from their own isolated nails. Outside, the evening sky is dark and fat with waiting rain, but the river is low and a little rain will be welcome. The day's fishing is done, but the conversation has just begun. It's time to talk about steelhead.

All up and down this dark river on this dark night there are other fishermen in other cabins just settling into their fire-warmed chairs and getting ready to talk about the same thing. After all, that's what fishermen do at night along any river when the steelhead are running. They talk about fish and fishing and other fishermen and other rivers and usually they complain that things just aren't as good as they used to be, and usually they are right. Then they'll yawn and stretch and go to bed early so they can be out on the river again at dawn, hoping that perhaps for just one day things might again be as good as they ever were. At least that is how it is on the North Fork of the Stillaguamish, my home river.

I have written often of the North Fork in other venues, of its early history and the magnificent run of wild summer steelhead that returned to Deer Creek, its major tributary; of how the North Fork became a special place in the minds, memories, and lore of Northwest anglers, the nearest thing to a western fishing shrine; of the brutal rape of the Deer Creek watershed by loggers, the subsequent deterioration of its summer steelhead run nearly to the point of extinction, and the resulting decline of the fishery, and finally of how I came into ownership of Bucktail Camp, Enos Bradner's old North Fork fishing cabin, just in time to witness the acceleration of that decline.

That was fifteen years ago, and the decision to acquire Bucktail Camp represented the solution to an interesting dilemma. At the time I was not especially concerned about the fishing in the North Fork—it still seemed good enough then—and my family had fallen in love with Bucktail Camp. But I realized that if I bought the place it would mean a dramatic change in my angling lifestyle. I had spent the better part of a decade barnstorming around the Northwest's steelhead rivers, fishing wherever and whenever I wished, and had grown to enjoy the variety and challenge of prospecting in so many different waters. I knew that ownership of Bucktail Camp would tie me to the North Fork in such a way that it would reduce, if not altogether eliminate, the chance to fish other rivers as often as I liked.

That was the heart of the dilemma and it was a matter I pondered at considerable length, mentally weighing the pros and cons of acquisition versus continuation of the free-spirited angling life I had led. In the end the allure of Bradner's old place and the lore associated with it, plus the assurance of access to some

of the very best water on the North Fork, was simply too much to resist, and we bought the place. The results of that decision were just as I had anticipated: I began spending more and more of my time on the North Fork to the exclusion of other rivers, and my days as a nomadic angler came swiftly to an end.

But I also found that I did not regret it at all, for I soon discovered the infinite pleasure and satisfaction that comes from getting to know a river on the most intimate terms. I learned the North Fork—or at least that portion of it near my cabin—far better than I had ever known any other river, well enough to recognize each small change in it from day to day, week to week, and season to season: subtle shifts in the places where steelhead held, the spots where it was always safe to wade and those where sometimes it was not; the areas I could reach with a fly and the areas that were beyond reach or not worth reaching; the correct approach, the proper casting angle—all the little details that usually defied discovery on streams I fished less often. Other rivers had been my acquaintances, but the North Fork became my friend.

In the early years of our ownership of Bucktail Camp the river also provided many memorable and exciting moments. I remember the day of the picnic at Lew Bell's cabin, a half-mile below Bucktail Camp, and how after lunch Lew and I went out on the river together and I quickly hooked a fish in the pool we called the Lower Rip-Rap. The steelhead took the fly halfway down a long stretch of broken water and jumped four times in succession, so high that it seemed to be looking down at me from the apex of every leap. It fought well, aided by the swift current, and when I finally steered it to the beach I could scarcely believe it was only a four-pound fish, a typical Deer Creek native steelhead, slim and streamlined, steel blue along its back with just the first touch of rainbow color showing on its sides.

I remember too my first fish from the Cliff Pool, a handsome piece of water where a long riffle breaks into a wide mysterious-looking pool with complex braided currents that eventually join to flow along the edge of a steep, water-battered bedrock wall. It had the look of a classic steelhead pool, but always before it had disappointed me—partly because its complicated currents made it difficult to get a decent drift with a fly, partly because it rarely seemed to hold a fish even though it looked as if it should. But one day it did, a beautiful steelhead that took my fly well up in the pool, just below the riffle, and led me on a long, merry chase far downstream until I was finally able to subdue it. The fish was as clean and bright as the sunlight glancing off the river, and I laid my rod next to it and saw that it reached past the ring of tape I had placed to mark the thirty-inch point on the rod.

One evening my son, Randy, was wading a slow, deep portion of the river just at dark when he heard what sounded like the rise of an enormous steelhead just downstream. He cast toward the sound and something big and powerful seized his fly with such strength that it caught him off balance and toppled him into the stream. He came up sputtering, waders full of water, and discovered he had hooked a large and very angry beaver. Fortunately, the leader soon parted and the beaver and Randy went their separate ways, each properly indignant over the experience.

Another time Lew Bell and I were hiking downstream after fishing a remote part of the river when we rounded a bend and came upon two young women swimming nude in a placid pool. They saw us, smiled and waved, and Lew and I stood there looking back dumbly, I suppose with our jaws somewhere down around our wading shoes. We watched a while until finally Lew said, "They look like they've already spawned," and we waved back at them and went on our way.

One sweltering August day I was invited by Chris Crabtree, who owned another cabin near Bucktail Camp, to go with him to try a stretch of river farther downstream than I normally fished. We parked his car off the road and walked across a half-mile-wide alfalfa field that reeked unbearably from a fresh application of cow manure. At the far side of the field was a nearly impenetrable thicket of blackberry vines; someone in the past had hacked a narrow passage through the thicket, but the vines had quickly reclaimed the opening and we were forced to hold our waders above our heads to keep them from being punctured by the thorns while we pushed our way through.

The river, when we finally reached it, brought instant relief from the reek of manure, the grasping thorns and the heat, and we entered it eagerly. The water was interesting and we took turns fishing our way downstream until we came to a huge pool, several hundred yards long and at least fifty yards wide, with the deepest water flowing along the foot of a steep clay bank on the opposite side. Here was a pool big enough to occupy the better part of a summer afternoon, and we fished it together for nearly an hour, but without seeing a sign of any fish. At length Chris decided to try the next pool downstream; I thought about going with him, but decided to stay where I was because I didn't think I had yet covered the big pool as thoroughly as it deserved.

A short while later my persistence was rewarded by the sight of a big steelhead rolling in deep water against the far bank. The fish was in a difficult spot, almost beyond the reach of a double-haul cast and lying just below an ugly snag. I started wading into position to begin casting and the fish obligingly rolled a second time, enabling me to get an even better fix on its location. Double-hauling for all I was worth, I managed to get my fly over the spot without hanging up on the snag, but nine or ten casts brought no response, so I clipped off the bright fly I had been using and replaced it with a dark one. Two or three casts later the fish hit the fly with one of the hardest strikes I have ever had from any steelhead; the rod tip was jerked savagely under water, the grip almost torn from my grasp, and the fish was instantly on the reel, tearing off line.

Perhaps it was the unexpected vigor of the strike, or maybe it was just general ineptitude on my part, but for whatever reason I overreacted and came up sharply on the rod while the fish was still in the early moments of its angry run. A flailing strand of broken leader came sailing out of the water and the fish—free again but with my fly still stuck in its jaw—leaped twice on its way out of the pool, down through the long tail-out and into the next pool where I could see Chris fishing in the distance.

Neither of us saw another fish for the rest of the afternoon. Some days are like that.

In the span of years over which I have come to know the North Fork, the most obvious changes to it have been physical in nature. When we bought the cabin it had a fine, wide gravel bar out in front, and for most of the first decade of our ownership the river added to it generously. Soil formed on top of the gravel, grass and wildflowers grew up in the soil, then willows and alders and cottonwoods took root and flourished and it seemed the place was well on its way to becoming a permanent part of the landscape. Then, just a few years ago, the river suddenly turned on its creation and started rapidly undoing what it had done, eroding away the soil and gravel and taking great chunks and gulps from the bar until now it is scarcely half its former size. But the river also has given compensation by carving out a long, swift, fish-holding run just downstream, and now there is twice as much water to fish as there was before.

So the river giveth and the river taketh away. And that is surely one of the most interesting things about having a place on a river—you can never be certain from one season to the next just exactly how much of a place you are going to have.

About the same time it started gnawing away at our gravel bar, the river also began to bring us increasing loads of silt from a great slide on logged-over land along upper Deer Creek. The fragile soils of the upper Deer Creek watershed had been slipping and sliding away for years after being damaged by logging and slash burning, and the creek and the river below it always had been muddy and unfishable after rain. But the slide was not dependent on rain; it was fed by underground seepage, which meant that it pumped a continuous flow of silt into Deer Creek. The creek obediently carried it down to the river and the river carried it all the way to the sea, and soon a great stain of silt could be seen spreading out from the river into the formerly clear waters of Port Susan Bay in Puget Sound.

For nearly three years the slide kept the North Fork below Deer Creek perpetually cloudy, rarely clear enough to fish with a fly. On those few occasions when it was fishable I was grateful I had learned the river so well—I knew all the dips and swells of its bottom and the location of its hidden boulders so that I could wade the river safely even when it was so dirty the bottom was invisible in water that was only knee deep.

On those days when the river was marginally fishable, we

began to see other alarming changes in its character. Silt began drifting up behind rocks and in pockets, and some of these drifts were so deep and of such a thin consistency that if an angler blundered into one of them in the cloudy water he would begin sinking into it, as if it were quicksand. This added a new element of difficulty to wading the once-friendly North Fork.

Of course the silt meant there was little likelihood of survival for the offspring of any fish that tried to spawn below the slide, and it also meant suffocation and death for much of the insect population of the North Fork. The disappearance of insect life cut sharply into the supply of food available for juvenile steelhead and salmon and all the other creatures that had relied upon it—the swallows that fed on the daytime hatches and the bats that dined in the evening—and upset the entire food chain for that portion of the river.

Silt also filled the bed of the river to such an extent that it could no longer carry the same volume of water as before, and winter floods—always a problem—became much worse. Several times in the early years of our ownership of Bucktail Camp water had seeped through the dike and flooded our cabin, but because it came from seepage the water always had been clear and the floods had subsided with little damage. But after silt filled the riverbed, dirty water began spilling over the top of the dike each time the river flooded, and when the floods subsided they left thick layers of silt both inside and outside the cabin. The silt deposits were like freshly poured cement when they were wet and like concrete when they dried, defying removal with anything except a chisel.

Those were sad times on the North Fork. It appeared the river might be unfishable for years to come, and the destruction of Deer Creek and its spawning and rearing water offered little hope that steelhead would be available even if the river should clear up enough to fish. True, there was still good fishing available for hatchery-bred steelhead in the North Fork above Deer Creek, but that offered little consolation to us who had staked our fortunes on the lower river. Nevertheless, faced with the ceaseless flow of slate gray silt from Deer Creek, I began spending more and more fishing time on the upper North Fork and the neighboring upper Sauk.

The North Fork of the Stillaguamish and the upper Sauk River are juxtaposed in a curious fashion. The North Fork heads in the hills north of the town of Darrington and flows south a short distance, then makes a nearly right-angle turn and flows west toward Puget Sound; the Sauk heads in the mountains south of Darrington and flows almost due north to its junction with the Skagit River. For some distance the two rivers flow parallel to each other but in opposite directions, separated only by a low divide. Geological evidence suggests they may once have been the same river, with the Sauk flowing into the North Fork before mudflows from a prehistoric volcanic eruption caused it to change its course.

But if they were once the same they are very different rivers now. The North Fork heads at a lower elevation and is fed mostly by springs and rainfall and is by far the more gentle of the two, well settled into its channel and surprisingly warm and docile in summer. The Sauk, on the other hand, receives much of its water from high-elevation snowfields and glaciers; it is a truly wild river, often flooding violently in winter and undergoing radical shifts in its restless channel, and even on sweltering afternoons in late August its current remains swift and its water shockingly cold. Sometimes I would fish both of them on the same day, and they offered a pleasant contrast to each other—especially to an angler who had grown tired of trying to wade and fish in silt.

One result of spending more time on the upper North Fork and the Sauk was that I became much better acquainted with the surrounding countryside and its colorful people. The town of Darrington and the upper valley of the North Fork are the centers of an area heavily populated by transplanted North Carolina Tarheels and their descendants, mostly people who came to the Northwest to work in its woods or its mills. Along with them they brought many traits and customs, including a certain clannishness and general suspicion of outsiders, especially bureaucrats of any stripe; boundless loyalty and friendship to anyone they trust; a fondness for moonshine whiskey and bluegrass music; and a general disregard for rules and regulations, especially those pertaining to fish and game.

The upper valley of the North Fork was a good place for them to settle. It lies well away from the main north-south transportation corridors of the Puget Sound Basin, sufficiently off the beaten track that for a good many years people who lived there could do pretty much as they pleased without fear of government bureaucrats looking over their shoulders. Darrington itself sits in a spectacular setting at the base of Whitehorse Mountain, a magnificent, soaring, glacier-tipped crag that seems to rise almost vertically from the valley floor. Other mountains rise to the north and east, all thickly carpeted with stands of fir and cedar—potential fodder for the saws at the Darrington mill, the reason for Darrington's existence.

But despite its idyllic setting, life in Darrington never has been easy. Jobs in the woods or the mill are always hard and uncertain. The work itself is difficult and dangerous and employment is subject to the periodic whims and fluctuations of the timber market—or, more recently, to increasing public opposition to the logging of diminishing stands of old-growth timber. Labor problems also seem endemic to the industry, and a long strike at the Darrington mill left a lot of empty storefronts in a town that never had very many stores to begin with. But the folks in Darrington are painfully familiar with hard times, and whenever they come around, some local residents fall back on a long tradition of subsistence hunting and fishing. In other words, they poach.

A certain amount of poaching always goes on along the North Fork or in the Sauk, but most of the time it is done more or less surreptitiously—perhaps a little nighttime netting, or a stick of dynamite thrown into a remote pool, or someone sneaking through the brush for a chance to shoot or spear a fish, the sort of thing that unfortunately happens on most Northwest rivers. But when times are tough in Darrington, the poachers grow bold and come right out in daylight.

Ted Rogowski and I saw graphic evidence of this one day when we went up to the Sauk to search for steelhead. It was late in the season and there were salmon in the river along with the steelhead; during the day we had seen some run-of-the-river sockeye in their bright spawning colors and several big dark king salmon forcing their way upstream through the shallow riffles. At the end of the day we were hiking downstream to the place where we had left the car when we came upon a remarkable sight: A short, stocky man stood on the edge of a gravel bar, casting awkwardly with a stout fiberglass rod rigged with a heavy monofilament line and what appeared to be a pair of heavy battery cable clamps attached to a large set of treble hooks. We watched as he lobbed this cumbersome affair into the current, then quickly reeled in while simultaneously jerking the stout rod up and down in an obvious effort to snag a fish.

Ted and I started forward, ready to give the man a good talking-to, but before we could reach him he cast again and this time he struck something. He reared back forcefully on the rod, which was about the size and shape of a cue stick and scarcely bent under the pressure, and the river exploded into froth. We watched in amazement as he took a few frantic turns on his reel, then threw down the rod and launched himself full-length into the river to tackle a big king salmon that was thrashing around in the shallows. The weighted set of treble hooks was buried deeply in the salmon's side.

Locked together in the poacher's embrace, man and fish rolled over twice in the shallow water; then the poacher managed to get a hand inside the salmon's gills and staggered to his feet, dripping from head to foot. The salmon, which looked to be about twenty-five pounds, writhed in his grasp, streaming blood from the wound in its side and pouring fresh eggs from its vent. He held it up proudly, splashed ashore and came right up to us, still holding the fish, and I noted he was missing several fingers from each

hand—the certain sign of a man who has spent most of his life working in the woods or the mills. Glaring defiantly, the poacher opened his mouth to speak, exposing us to a gust of vile breath and a glimpse of bad teeth that looked like an uneven row of tombstones with some kicked over.

"What else am I gonna do?" he asked. "I got eleven kids and no job."

I thought of suggesting birth control, but somehow it didn't seem appropriate under the circumstances.

Poaching is not the only illegal activity that goes on in the hills around Darrington. Tradition has it that in the old days there was a moonshine still hidden behind nearly every stump, and revenue agents ventured into the upper valley only at their peril. But those days are long past—or so everyone thought until just recently, when state and federal agents busted one of the biggest stills on record near Darrington and seized a goodly share of its output. The latter was deemed extremely smooth and powerful—even the arresting officers testified to that, for they apparently paused to sample some before they hustled the still's owner off to jail. The owner turned out to be a man of some local stature and influence, and when word of his arrest got around, public respect for him increased to the point that he probably could have run for election to any office in the valley and won easily.

Perhaps a moonshine still would explain the presence of an unusual sign I came across one day while fishing on the upper North Fork, or maybe it was just an expression of general unfriendliness on the landowner's part. I had left my truck at a highway turnout near the river and fished downstream for nearly a mile, wading the entire distance because the river was bordered on either side by steep banks topped with thick brush and fallen timber. Rather than wade back the whole way against the current, I decided instead to cut through the woods to the highway and try to thumb a ride back to my truck.

I scrambled up the steep bank, found a deer trail at the top, and followed it through the woods to a broad pasture. A few cows were grazing in a far corner of the pasture but they paid no attention as I crossed to a fence line on the far side. Beyond the fence was another stretch of thick woods and beyond that I could hear the noise of cars and trucks passing on the highway, probably no more than a hundred yards away. But the fence was new, with strands of barbed wire strung closely and tightly together, and I could not find a place where it looked safe to climb over or under it without tearing my waders. So I started walking along the fence, feeling certain that if I followed it far enough I would find a gate.

Sure enough, after a couple of hundred yards I saw a gate ahead with a road beyond it curving into the woods toward the highway. As I got closer I also noticed a house set well back in the woods on the other side of the road.

And then I saw the sign. It was nailed to a tree, just on the other side of the gate, a large sheet of whitewashed plywood with big red letters painted on it. It said:

FRIEND, IF I SEE YOU,

I'LL SHOOT TO KILL

I stood there and stared at the sign for a long while. It might be a joke, but I remembered I'd heard a lot of stories about fishermen who had been shot at along this stretch of the river.

I looked from the sign to the house. I couldn't see anyone, but I wondered if someone there could see me, if perhaps at that very moment someone was standing behind one of the dark upstairs windows, squinting through a telescopic sight with the cross-hairs lined up on the lamb's wool patch on my fishing vest.

Cars rushed by on the highway a hundred yards away and I looked back at the sign and wondered if I should chance it. A little breeze stirred the nearby leaves and made rustling sounds back in the woods and I made up my mind.

Wading back upstream wasn't quite as difficult as I'd thought it would be, but it was late and I was tired by the time I reached the truck.

My exile to the upper North Fork and the neighboring Sauk lasted the better part of the three seasons during which most of the time it was impossible to fish in the river below Deer Creek. But every cloud has a silver lining, or so it is said, and the silver lining in the cloud of silt issuing from Deer Creek turned out to be a growing sense of public fury. The slide in the upper water-shed was only the most visible manifestation of a generation of abuse and mismanagement, and the declining fishery, worsening floods, and deteriorating physical environment aroused public indignation and drew the attention of local newspapers. Responding to this increasingly squeaky wheel of public sentiment, agencies of the federal, state, and county governments joined with representatives of fishing and environmental groups and local Indian tribes to form a committee called the Deer Creek Policy Group, with the objective of trying to solve some of the massive problems in the watershed.

Operating on the philosophy that there was nothing to be gained by pointing fingers of blame at those who were at fault for past abuses, the group set aside the differences of its members and tried to plan strategies to halt the decline of Deer Creek and begin some sort of rehabilitation program. As a result of these discussions, the U.S. Forest Service declared a moratorium on future logging of its remaining timberlands in the Deer Creek drainage, and the state Department of Natural Resources agreed to substantial concessions on some of its future logging plans. These were obvious and much-belated steps, but they still represented a significant change in policy for two agencies traditionally subservient to the interests of the logging industry.

The Department of Natural Resources also made substantial and costly attempts to stem the flow of silt from the slide on upper Deer Creek. All of these turned out badly, but in the end nature finally intervened where man had failed: In 1987, when the spring runoff subsided, anglers were surprised to see Deer Creek and the lower North Fork suddenly flowing clear again after nearly three years of continuous turbidity. It was soon discovered that the source of groundwater seepage feeding the upstream slide had dried up, at least temporarily, thus ending the steady flow of silt into Deer Creek. No one could predict when or if the seepage might begin again, but the North Fork remained clear all that summer and for the two summers that followed, allowing fishermen once again to return to its waters.

During those years the river also began the long, slow process of cleansing itself. While vast pockets of silt remain, a few have been flushed away—enough to make wading pleasant once again, or to provide a few more sheltering spots for resting steelhead.

Last season also brought a great explosion in the population of caddisflies, more than anyone had seen for a long time, a hopeful sign that life is returning to those areas of the river cleansed of suffocating silt.

Meanwhile, the work of restoration has begun on the upper Deer Creek watershed. Silt barriers have been installed, new foliage has been planted to stabilize the fragile streambank soils, and boulders have been placed in the streams to try to restore a proper pool-to-riffle ratio. Some of this work has been financed by the government, but much of it was paid for with funds raised through the untiring efforts of Alec Jackson, perhaps the only true hero of the Deer Creek saga. Jackson, representing the fly-fishing community on the Deer Creek Policy Group, worked to the point of exhaustion and endangered health to prevent more logging of the watershed, and tapped every conceivable source to raise funds for rehabilitation. Such dedication is all the more remarkable in light of the fact that Jackson and everyone who worked with him were aware that their efforts were being made mostly on behalf of future generations. For no matter how much money is spent or how much effort is expended, the full restoration of Deer Creek is likely to take longer than the lifespan of anyone now living.

Even with restoration, there is no assurance that the native steelhead will ever return. The wild run of Deer Creek steelhead was already at a critically low ebb when the slide began covering what little remained of the downstream spawning and rearing water, and now only a few stretches in the uppermost reaches of the watershed remain suitable for spawning. Even these waters may have been inaccessible to adult steelhead during the years of massive silt flows—not that it would have mattered greatly, for it appears likely that a high percentage of the few fish returning in those years were captured in Indian gill nets downstream.

The netting, legalized by federal court ruling, is supposed to be regulated to allow proper spawning escapement, but the regulations have never been properly enforced. Many untended nets have been found anchored or adrift in the lower river, and these abandoned nets kill steelhead just as efficiently as those tended carefully by their owners on a daily basis. The Indian fishermen surely bear no share of blame for the abuse and mismanagement that brought the Deer Creek steelhead run to its lowest ebb, but they may well share the responsibility for giving it the final push over the precipice of extinction.

Hatchery-reared steelhead still return to the North Fork in fair abundance, but their passage through the waters below Deer Creek is a hurried one. In the past few seasons I have found a few of them in the pools around Bucktail Camp early in the summer and again sometimes late in the fall, but from mid-July through mid-September the lower North Fork now seems mostly empty of the gleaming steelhead that once waited restlessly in the pools below Deer Creek.

The North Fork also is vulnerable to other environmental problems. Most serious of these is the threat of metastasizing urban sprawl caused by rapid population growth in the Puget Sound Basin. Already the ugly symptoms are starting to show in the lower valley and their spread upstream undoubtedly will be accelerated by a massive and unnecessary expansion of the highway that parallels the North Fork. The highway project, overwhelmingly opposed by local residents, was rammed through by an unresponsive state transportation agency interested only in perpetuating itself and spending as much public money as possible.

So it is obvious now that the best days of the North Fork have come and gone, probably never to return, and that is why the anglers who live along and love this river now spend many of their evenings in nostalgic conversations about the way things used to be. And although their numbers are fewer now—and perhaps that in itself is something of a blessing—there are still some anglers who continue to fish the lower river faithfully, who are glad to see it running clear again below Deer Creek even if it is often empty of fish.

I am one of those, and I still spend countless summer hours wading the long-familiar drifts or trudging the well-worn paths along the gravel bars. These days the signs of steelhead are few and far between, but each pool still holds precious memories that are somehow renewed and refreshed each time I return to it. Along with the memories, I still enjoy the feel of the river around me, the sounds of its restless passage, the sight of the eagles and ospreys and kingfishers and herons that are as persistent in their fishing habits as I am in mine. Though fish may be few, I never leave the river feeling unsatisfied or unfulfilled.

In particular I remember a late dog-day summer afternoon I spent on the river last season. For six weeks I had seen no fish and I did not expect to see any on this day, although the river was up slightly and seemed a bit more lively after a hard rain several days before. A few humpback salmon had come in, somehow escaping the nets downstream and in salt water, and these were playing and splashing at the head of one of my favorite pools. The day was clear and hot, but when I looked upstream I could see thunderheads building far up the valley, steamy-white and boiling up to block the view of Whitehorse Mountain. I spent the afternoon fishing easily and comfortably through all the old familiar places, feeling a pleasant synchronization with the rhythm of the river and enjoying the satisfaction that always comes from fishing well even when there are no fish about—which, as I had expected, was once again the case.

I fished until evening, enjoying the growing coolness of the calm air and the peaceful river and feeling completely in harmony with all my surroundings. The sun made me squint as it sank toward the horizon of the western hills, and forced me to focus downstream so that it was quite a long time before I happened to glance up the valley in the other direction. There I saw the thunderheads that had been building all afternoon were now spilling swiftly down the valley, and as I continued fishing I kept looking over my shoulder to watch their rapid progress. No longer were they white and billowing; now they were dark and red in the light of the setting sun, and before long I could hear the rumble and mutter of deep thunder somewhere behind them.

Down the valley they rushed until they were nearly overhead, a great churning swollen curtain of cloud, swelling swiftly toward the sunset that lit them brightly and made them the color of blood. Suddenly their reflected light was everywhere, and I found myself standing in a river of blood, surrounded by blood-drenched rocks and trees with motionless blood-stained leaves under a lowering blood-red sky, and I stopped fishing and stood transfixed at the eerie sight.

Then just as quickly the sun dipped and the light died, the color drained out of everything, the river darkened, and the clouds became ugly and gray. I fished on until it was too dark to see, then started the long crossing back to my cabin while the storm growled and grumbled overhead and spat out a single long shaft of ragged lightning to briefly light my way.

Afterward I wondered if the illusion of wading hip-deep in a blood-red river might offer some sort of natural metaphor for the tragedy of the North Fork, Deer Creek, and the native steelhead run, for truly it seems all three have been bled until there is little or no life left in them.

But I will continue fishing the North Fork, though with a mind more full of memories than of hope. In spite of all that has happened, there may yet still be a chance that a few steelhead will come my way and remind me briefly of the way things used to be, and if that should happen I will return each precious fish gently to the river and wish it Godspeed on its spawning mission. Even if it does not happen, I will go on fishing, for I am not yet ready to give up. I love the North Fork, and I will be faithful to it—as only a fisherman can be to his home river.

# 8 | THE STEELHEAD
# ALSO RISES

Like most steelhead fly fishermen of my generation, I learned to fish with wet flies and sinking lines. Conventional wisdom—if that is what it was—held that fast-sinking lines and sometimes even weighted flies were necessary to "get down to the fish," which always were presumed to be pressing their bellies into the rocks at the bottom of the very deepest pools, even in summer, and were thought unwilling to move very far, if at all, to take a fly.

This made steelhead fly fishing a ritual where nearly everything took place out of the angler's view; his part in it was to cast, perhaps to mend his line so that the fly would sink even deeper than it would otherwise, then simply sit back, wait, and hold on in the hope that somewhere, far down below the swirling bright surface of the river, a steelhead would see the fly and take it.

Another aspect of this traditional view of steelhead fly fishing was that only bright flies would do—the brighter the better, and if they also happened to resemble drifting salmon eggs, well that was better still—although that had begun to change a little by the time I began fishing seriously for steelhead.

When all these things were taken together it was obvious that steelhead fly fishermen had simply imitated the tactics of bait fishermen, who had developed their methods long before fly fishing began to grow popular in the Pacific Northwest. That tradition, plus the limitations of early fly-fishing tackle—it was difficult back in the days of silk fly lines to fish flies on or just under the surface because the lines became waterlogged so easily—made the sinking fly the method of choice for many years.

It was still the preferred method when I took up the sport. At the time local anglers weren't giving much thought to the idea that steelhead could be caught on flies in any other way—on dry flies, for example, or on sparsely dressed low-water patterns fished in the surface film or just under it. About the only exception to this conventional line of thought was expressed in the writings of Roderick Haig-Brown, who had observed not only that steelhead could be taken on dry flies but that under some circumstances floating patterns were even more effective than wet flies.

Nobody doubted Haig-Brown's word on the matter, but everyone knew he lived and fished on Vancouver Island where the rivers were rumored to be literally paved with steelhead. Not only that, but Vancouver Island steelhead were thought to be somehow different from their mainland counterparts; they were said to be free-rising, eager, active fish, while those in the mainland rivers were so stubborn and dour that on some days it seemed one might as well be casting to a school of turnips.

I could attest to that, having once located a large steelhead resting in a pool and fished for it nearly an hour, during which time I was able to refine the length of the cast and gauge the speed of the current to the point that several times I was literally able to bounce my fly off the steelhead's snout, but the fish remained totally indifferent all the while, never once giving any sign of acknowledgement to the numerous fly patterns I offered it.

Even my mentors, Ralph Wahl and Enos Bradner, fished almost exclusively with wet flies. I had heard Ralph speak of taking steelhead on dry flies but never saw him do it, and if Brad ever used a dry fly for steelhead I never heard him say so. So I fished as they did—in fact, as nearly everyone did in those days—but with an increasing sense that something important was missing from my fishing experience. During my early years as a trout fishermen I had grown to love using the dry fly and to prefer it over any other method; the sight of a trout rising to a floating fly had become for me the most rewarding part of angling, even more than the fight that followed, and I could only imagine how exciting it would be to see a large steelhead do the same thing.

So it was only a matter of time until I began to try. Several times when circumstances seemed right I switched from sinking to floating lines and a dry fly to cast over steelhead I had seen and knew were there. In each case I relied on a conventional trout-style upstream approach and drag-free float, but never once did I inveigle a fish to rise, so I never developed any confidence in the method. And confidence, as every experienced angler knows, is the most important thing in fly fishing; there is a sort of natural law that if you lack confidence in a method you will never try it long enough for it to prove itself, and if you don't give it the opportunity to prove itself you will never develop confidence in it. It's a Catch-22 situation, and in my case it meant that after a few casts with a dry fly I would usually give up and change back to a sinking line and wet fly.

In the end it was Walt Johnson and Ralph Wahl who led me to my first steelhead on a dry fly. Walt provided the method and Ralph pinpointed the location of the fish, although in each case their actions were inadvertent.

I had run into Walt one evening while he was fishing one of the larger pools on the North Fork of the Stillaguamish. It's always pleasant and instructive to watch a master fly fisher at his craft, so I sat down on a handy log and settled back to see how Walt fished the pool. At first I thought he was using conventional wet-fly technique, throwing a long line quartering downstream, but to my surprise I soon noticed he was casting a floating line instead of a sinker. At the end of the line was something even more surprising, a floating fly that scratched the surface of the river in an unnatural arc, then dipped under at the end of each cast. Walt told me it was the motion of the floating fly, so unlike a conventional drag-free float, that seemed to attract the attention of steelhead. Often, he said, a fish would pick up the fly halfway through its swing and follow it until it dipped under the surface, then take it. I can't remember now if he was using a riffle hitch on the fly, but the effect was the same.

This immediately struck me as a technique worth trying. I had long ago discovered that a skated dry fly was highly effective in provoking resident trout to rise, and this seemed like the same thing—the combination of a quartering downstream cast and the river's current causing the fly to skate over the surface as the line straightened out below the caster. I had been schooled so thoroughly in the doctrine of the upstream dry-fly approach that I had never seriously considered the notion of fishing a floating fly downstream, and the very idea seemed a bit heretical; but if an angler of Walt Johnson's stature was willing to try it, then there was no reason why I should not be willing, too. So I filed the idea away in the back of my mind, waiting for the right combination of circumstances to try it.

Those circumstances presented themselves one morning when I bumped into Ralph Wahl on a trail along the river near the Elbow Hole of the North Fork. Ralph said he had been fishing farther downstream and had seen a steelhead roll at the foot of a slick; he had cast to it a number of times but the fish had not taken. I knew exactly the spot he meant and knew also it would be an ideal place to try a dry fly fished downstream. But I thought it also would be a good idea to wait a while and rest the pool before I tried it, so I fussed around camp impatiently for a couple of hours, then finally went out in the early afternoon, armed with a fly rod rigged with a floating line.

I had tied some flies for just this type of occasion, and the pattern I chose was a sort of giant version of the Adams dry fly. Tied on a #6 low-water long-shanked Atlantic salmon hook, it had the familiar gray dubbed-fur body and mixed brown and grizzly hackles of the Adams, but the divided hackle-point wings of the traditional pattern had been replaced by a single upright deer-hair wing. I knotted one of these flies to a six-pound test tippet on the end of a twelve-foot leader, greased it thoroughly, then waded out slowly and cautiously to the head of the slick.

It took a few casts to figure out how and when to mend the line in order to keep enough tension on it so that the fly would skate temptingly through its semicircular path, but after a little while I got the hang of it and began to fish slowly and carefully down the slick to the point where Ralph had seen the fish.

Then it happened: I made the downstream-quartering cast, mended line twice, and watched the fly plow its little furrow in the surface until it suddenly vanished in a quiet rise. The take was so gentle and delicate it might have been made by a wary brown trout sipping a mayfly spinner, but it was quickly followed by a great boil on the surface and then floating line was whistling out through the rod guides as the hooked steelhead raced downstream.

It was not an especially big fish—only about five pounds as I recall—and although it ran well and jumped several times, its fight was nothing beyond the ordinary. But there are no words to describe the elation I felt when I finally eased that handsome silver steelhead onto the Stillaguamish gravel and saw my floating fly stuck firmly in the corner of its jaw. Though the method was unorthodox, here at least was proof that steelhead *could* be caught on a floating fly—even dour mainland-river steelhead.

That success triggered the beginnings of confidence. By itself it was not enough to convince me I should begin fishing the dry fly as a regular practice, especially to begin fishing it blindly without being certain of the presence of fish, but it did give me faith enough to use the dry fly more often and to persevere with it in situations where I might otherwise have given up on it earlier. And of course that had the double effect of increasing my chances for success and improving my skill so that it was not very long before another success was forthcoming, and then another and another.

It was a gradual, evolutionary process, but after several seasons I found myself using the dry fly not just most of the time, but nearly all of the time, and agreeing with Haig-Brown that under many circumstances it was a far more effective method than the wet fly, at least for summer steelhead. In reaching this point I had also managed to break through the hidebound tradition that constrained my earlier efforts, and this led to many refinements in method. I added the riffle hitch as a standard tactic, designed fly patterns specifically to take advantage of it, and experimented with other floating-line methods and approaches.

The riffle hitch is a simple method of changing the action of a floating fly. The fly is first tied to the leader in conventional fashion, but then a pair of hitches are taken in the tippet, forming a loop that is then slipped over the eye of the fly and cinched tight—usually around the base of the fly's head, but sometimes farther back, just forward of or just behind the wing. The result is that the leader joins the fly at an angle, and this off-center pull means that when the fly is on the water it always rides at an angle to the direction of the current. This causes it to skate across the surface, causing enough of a disturbance or wake to attract the attention of fish.

The key to making this work is to mend line properly so there is always tension on the line between the rod tip and the fly, and to tie the hitch so that the leader comes off the side of the fly facing the angler. If an angler changes sides of the river and forgets to change his riffle hitch, he'll end up with a fly that sinks instead of skates.

As it turned out, I was not alone in experimenting with the

riffle hitch and other dry-fly methods. A similar kind of angling ferment was going on all over the Pacific Northwest, stimulated largely by the work of Bill McMillan, whose experiments with the greased-line technique on southwest Washington rivers prompted emulation by many others. Articles published by McMillan also formed the nucleus of a growing body of literature on greased- or floating-line techniques, fly-pattern development, and other unconventional approaches to steelhead fly fishing, and McMillan deserves much of the credit for having fomented what has become a renaissance in Northwest angling methods over the past decade.

These developments have been very good for steelhead fly fishing, and on an individual and personal level they also have made the sport a much more satisfying one for me—for now it has become a wholly visual experience. I am convinced that the sight of a big steelhead lunging through the surface in pursuit of a floating fly is the absolute pinnacle of angling excitement; nothing could be more thrilling, more hair-raising, more breathtaking or heart-pounding than that, and I would willingly trade a half-dozen fish on the beach for the sight of a single one rising to a high-riding riffle-hitched dry fly.

Most of my dry-fly fishing experience has been near my camp on the North Fork of the Stillaguamish, since that is where I have fished most often over the past fifteen years. And although the decline of the North Fork's fishery has meant fewer successes in recent years, the river has left me with a full measure of rich and rewarding memories.

Just above my cabin at Bucktail Camp is a stretch of water called the Pocket. When I first began fishing it there was a shallow riffle at its head, tapering quickly into a long, deep run against the south bank, narrow at its upper end but widening gradually downstream until it broke over the top of a giant submerged boulder. Behind the boulder was a patch of deep water; this was the Pocket, a perfect holding spot for steelhead and perhaps the most dependable piece of dry-fly water the North Fork had to offer. The wading there was comfortable and easy, the best water was well within casting range, and the current was just fast and smooth enough for a perfect swing with a riffle-hitched dry fly. Only in the very low water of late summer did the fishing become difficult, and then only because the current slowed to the point that it was hard to get a decent drift with the fly.

During its best years the Pocket yielded more fish than I have taken from any other pool on the North Fork. I soon developed a routine for fishing it, starting at the upper end of the run and covering the slot against the south bank where fish sometimes held when the water was high, then gradually working downstream—usually with rising hopes—to the point where little wrinkles on the surface marked the passage of the current over the submerged boulder. There I would brace myself for action, for that was the "sweet spot" of the run, the spot where a rise was almost certain to be forthcoming if one was to come at all.

Very often it did come. I would aim my cast so that the fly fell just short of the riprapped bank on the far side, then mend quickly upstream once or twice and hold the rod tip high to keep as much line off the water as I could, all the while intently watching the progress of my fly as it started its arc across the wrinkled surface, the riffle hitch causing it to leave a little V-shaped wake. Sometimes the fly wouldn't make it even halfway across the pool before a great rising wave would appear behind it, followed by a quick flash of silver; then the fly would disappear and I would find myself fast to a surprised and angry steelhead. But more often the fly would transcribe a full arc across the pool, etching its little wake into the slick surface, and come finally to rest directly downstream; and then the rise would come.

Sometimes a fish would roll at the fly in midstream and miss it, then continue to chase it all the way across the pool, often lunging two or three times more in its wild eagerness to capture the moving morsel, and of course these were the most exciting moments of all; at such times it was hard to tell which was more frantic, the fish or the fisherman.

The 1980 season was the best of any I have spent on the North Fork. The steelhead run that year for some reason was the largest in a human generation—old-timers said it was the best since the war—and much larger than any since. My fishing diary bears the record of twenty-nine steelhead risen to a dry fly that summer, most of them in the Pocket.

August 1 of that year was warm and muggy and I waited until evening to go out and fish the Pocket. I had fished only twenty minutes, hurrying through the upper part of the run to get down to the best water, and just as my riffle-hitched fly came for the first time over the rock that marks the threshold of the Pocket, a fish rose and took it solidly. The fish fought sullenly and it was nearly dark before I landed it, a typically handsome Deer Creek native steelhead of about four pounds that was quickly returned to the river. It was the beginning of four memorable days of fishing.

The next morning brought a weather change and a stubborn drizzle that continued throughout the day. I worked around camp until afternoon, then started fishing again in the Pocket and gave it a thorough going-over, but this time nothing came to my fly so I moved a little way downstream to the Stump Pool, a much larger piece of water. On one of my first casts into the upper end of the pool a steelhead rose and took the fly decisively, then turned and bolted downstream. A moment later it was gone and when I retrieved the fly I quickly learned the reason why: The fine-wire low-water hook was broken at the barb.

I replaced the fly and went on fishing. Not five minutes later another steelhead appeared behind the skating fly, then lunged and took it in a spectacular splashing rise. The fish ran into the backing several times, jumped four or five times, and generally gave a thoroughly determined account of itself before I beached it about a hundred yards below the spot where it had been hooked. It was a fish of hatchery origin, a short but heavily built hen steelhead of about six pounds.

The next morning was still overcast and misty, but the afternoon brought another change in the weather; the mist cleared away and the day turned hot and bright. I began fishing late in the morning, once again in the Pocket, and worked my way through the upper part of the run without a touch. But just as soon as I reached the little stretch of wrinkled water over the submerged boulder, my riffle-hitched fly was sucked under by a fish that turned out to be a bright, spirited little jack steelhead of about two and a half pounds.

That evening I rose another fish, a much bigger one that came out of the water in a spectacular head-and-tail rise and missed the fly—either that, or I missed the strike. Missed strikes are not uncommon in steelhead dry-fly fishing, and I had learned early

on that the most difficult thing about fishing a dry fly down-stream is resisting the impulse to raise the rod to set the hook in a rising fish—for to do so almost certainly means pulling the fly away from the fish. The proper technique is to lower the rod and give slack so the fish has an opportunity to keep the fly in its mouth; then the pressure of the current on the fly line usually will give the hook a firm lodgement in the corner of the steel-head's mouth. But after a lifetime of aggressively setting hooks in rising trout, it's very hard to learn to do precisely the opposite thing, and although I continually remind myself of the proper technique, I still often find myself reacting impulsively in the wrong way.

No more fish came to my fly that evening, but the next morning I went down to fish the Stump Pool again an hour before first light. I used up most of the hour and most of the pool without result, but just in the last moments of shadow, before morning sunlight fell upon the river, a steelhead rose and took my fly. It was a splendid fish that jumped five times in succession, each jump causing an eruption of spray that glistened like a shower of diamonds in the onrushing morning light. When I finally brought the fish to hand it proved to be another Deer Creek native, a bright native buck of about five pounds, and I noted in my diary that catching it was just about the most fun I'd ever had for getting up early.

Later that day I went up to the Deer Creek Riffle and began bouncing a riffle-hitched floater down the quick, ruffled currents at the head of the run. A steelhead soon came up through the fast water and seized the fly in a burst of spray, then turned away sharply and ran downstream. I waded out and followed it down into a quiet reach where I let the fish tire itself in a series of short runs, each turned back by the pressure of the rod and the drag of the reel. At length it turned wearily on its side and I brought it close enough to have a good look at it, judging its weight at eight or ten pounds. But just as I began leading it up to the beach it righted itself in a last-ditch effort, made a halfhearted run, and the hook pulled out.

Naturally I was disappointed, but the feeling didn't last long. On my way back downstream I stopped to fish the Pocket, and there, in the usual spot, I rose and hooked another good steelhead. This one looked to be about six or seven pounds and was obviously annoyed to find itself hooked. It ran quickly into the backing and I began to wade toward shore so I could follow, but my rod, which had been bent by the weight of the running fish, suddenly recoiled to its original shape like a bow after the release of an arrow. For an instant I thought the fish had broken the leader, but then I saw thin backing line trailing away from the reel and noticed my fly line floating downstream and realized the line-to-backing splice had broken.

I rushed forward through deep water to try to grasp the line, but the fish was still attached and had ideas of its own; it pulled the line rapidly away from me. I gave chase and finally caught the butt end of the line in my fingers, but the steelhead again quickly pulled it from my grasp. I lunged forward, caught the line again, and this time held on as tightly as I could. I could still feel the strong, lively weight of the steelhead at the other end and after quick consideration of all the possibilities I decided my only chance was to try to hand-line the fish while I waded slowly toward the beach. But the steelhead was still fresh and scarcely willing to abide such tactics; it ran again, forcing me to grip the line as hard as I could to keep from losing it, and the leader quickly parted. I thought I had experienced just about every way it was possible to lose a fish, but that was a new one for me.

Still, over a period of four days I had risen eight steelhead to dry flies, hooked seven and landed four—and with a little more luck I might have landed all of them. In a hard-fished river close to major urban areas, that is remarkable steelhead fishing by any standard.

There were other noteworthy days that summer. My diary for August 23 records that I was on the river at 6:30 A.M. but found a fisherman in every likely spot, which forced me to beat a frustrated retreat to the cabin for breakfast. It was nearly 9 A.M. before I went back out on the river and found the Pocket empty of other fishermen. I had fished out a cast in the usual spot over the big boulder and had just taken the first couple of pulls of the retrieve when I saw a splash at my fly and felt the weight of a fish.

The steelhead dogged it for a while, holding in the deep water behind the boulder, then started toward the beach as if about to surrender without a fight. Then abruptly it turned and ran strongly out into the center of the current, angling upstream. I was in a good position, below the fish, but the steelhead felt strong and heavy and I didn't want to put too much strain on the six-pound test leader.

The fight continued in such fashion for perhaps ten minutes. Each time I gained line the fish would take it away again in short, strong runs, never going far enough to reach the backing. Then suddenly it changed tactics and jumped twice, and I could see it was a good-size steelhead with a touch of color that indicated it had been in the river for a time.

After the double jump the fish resumed its former behavior and we rejoined the stubborn give-and-take battle over line. More than twenty minutes had elapsed from the time I hooked it until it finally capitulated and I was able to lead it up to a patch of sand on the riverbank. It was a handsome hook-jawed buck steelhead of about eight pounds, and I saw that my fly was stuck so securely in the gristle of its upper jaw that I could have safely played the fish all day.

Next morning I returned to the Pocket and rose and hooked a fish in almost exactly the same spot, except this one chased the fly nearly clear across the pool before taking it in a noisy, splashing rise. Like the one I had caught the day before, at first it held quietly in the deep water of the Pocket, then edged downstream a little way. Suddenly it burst out of the water in a spectacular end-swapping leap that sent spray flying to the farthest corners of the pool, revealing itself as larger than yesterday's fish, maybe twelve pounds in weight. It also had a long vivid white scar on the top of its head, perhaps the souvenir of an encounter with a seal.

After its single jump the fish moved upstream again, then reversed direction and started down. At first it moved slowly, then with increasing speed, and soon my reel was spinning freely and I was dashing through the shallows in pursuit. I followed the fish down through the quiet water below the Pocket, down through the tail-out of the pool, all the way down to a spot where the river divided around a small island with the current spilling swiftly over gravel terraces on either side. I tried desperately to turn it there and get it headed back upstream, but the fish was too strong; it bore away, reached the channel of swift water on the far side of the island, and headed down.

Again I followed, running and splashing my way down the gravelly run, rod held high, watching the broad silver shape of tl.e fish slide over the rocks ahead of me. Then the fish was out of the channel and into the deeper but still swift water of the Elbow Hole, and I began to sense that it was tiring. Twice I tried to lead it into the protected shallows at the edge of the Elbow Hole, but each time it turned into deeper water, still moving downstream.

Then we were out of the Elbow Hole and into the broad run below it, and I made a decision to try to land the fish at the foot of a little island there, at least 250 yards downstream from where I had hooked it. The fish finally seemed ready and I led it cautiously but firmly into quiet water, then up onto the sand where it lay on its side, half out of the water, gill plates rising and falling spasmodically in exhaustion. I stepped forward to claim my prize, but before I could reach it the fish gave one last sudden lurch and flopped back into the river; the quick movement pulled my rod tip down to the sand and jammed it there, creating just enough strain on the leader that the fly pulled out of the steelhead's jaw.

For a long moment the steelhead and I both stood frozen in a tableau, I crouching and staring down at the motionless fish in the quiet water at the foot of the island, the fish in turn staring back at me. Then, with a weary twitch of its broad tail, the steelhead moved away slowly and disappeared in the dark green depths of the river.

I suppose I should have been disappointed, but I can truthfully say that I was not. I had planned to release the fish in any case, but its way was better; the steelhead had regained its own freedom in a fair fight, having bested me in the last moves of a critical end game after one of most spectacular battles I'd ever had with any fish. It was a wonderful way to start the day—and my diary records that night I also won at poker.

Next morning I was out on the river again at 6 A.M. It was a perfect dawn, cool enough that tendrils of steam were rising gently from the river, clear except for a thin layer of cirrus hovering around the canine peaks of Whitehorse Mountain, small clouds forming cutthroat slashes backlit by the rising sun. Again I started in the Pocket but fished all the way through it without a single customer, so I changed flies and started in again. Once more I fished down to the familiar sweet spot of the pool and watched the riffle-hitched fly sweep across the wrinkled current. Suddenly there was a big dorsal fin behind it, looking for all the world like a small shark chasing the fly; then the fish caught up to the fly, there was a violent eruption, and I felt the weight of a steelhead.

Like most fish hooked in the Pocket, this one first held in the deep water, then slowly moved upstream a bit. Then came a short run, a cartwheeling leap, and a longer run directly upstream and well into the backing. With the assistance of the current I quickly recovered most of the line, but then the fish ran upstream a second time and took it all back out again. Once more I reeled in until most of the line was back on the reel, but then the fish turned suddenly and shot past me, heading downstream, and ran all the way out of the Pocket and halfway down to the island. I followed as best I could, but the fish made another long run, this time to the far side of the river, using the last of its strength in the process. Reeling until my arm ached, I forced it back and slowly led it to shallow water like a reluctant puppy brought to heel. It was a long, slim fish, a buck steelhead with a big kype and rose-colored gill plates. Randy, who had watched me land it, was waiting on the beach with a measuring tape and scale to record its vital statistics: twenty-nine and a half inches, nine and a half pounds.

The wonderful fishing held up into the fall, even though fall came early that year. My diary for September 6 speaks of a gray, blustery day with the hollow roar of wind in the firs and cottonwoods along the river and a steady rain of leaves falling into the river. The floating leaves made fishing difficult because the riffle-hitched dry fly found them constantly and hooked them.

The day brought the normal kind of rain, too. It came sporadically in hard, quick bursts, and there had been much of it all through the preceding week. The river had risen at least four feet and was only beginning to settle back into shape, still a foot higher than the last time I had fished it and carrying more than a trace of color.

Once again I started fishing at the head of the Pocket, putting on a dry fly with some doubt that fish would be able to see it in the slightly cloudy water. Those doubts were quickly dispelled; on my second cast the river erupted as if a stick of dynamite had exploded under the fly. Despite the violence of the rise, or perhaps because of it, the fish somehow missed the fly. But a few casts later it came again, far out of the water this time, and crashed down on the fly so hard it snatched the line from my grasp. By the time I regained control the fish was gone.

I fished through the rest of the Pocket without further action, then changed flies and waded back in for a second pass. This time, in the usual spot, a steelhead rose and missed the fly just as it finished its swing. Three casts later the fish came up again and this time took the fly firmly. It made a long initial run, then stopped and thrashed on the surface, whipping the water to a froth. That was but the opening round of a long struggle filled with advances and retreats on either side until finally I was able to land the fish at the edge of the near-side channel around the island below the Pocket. It was another buck steelhead, about eight pounds, showing color enough to indicate it had been in the river for a time and a crisscross pattern of fresh scars that indicated a narrow brush with a gill net.

Thinking I probably had milked the Pocket for all it was worth, I fished on down through the Elbow and into the Stump Pool. Halfway through that long pool a steelhead rose and took my fly in midcurrent and after a good scrap I landed it, another buck, this one about seven pounds, gleaming bright and fresh from the ocean. In less than three hours of fishing I had managed five rises, hooked three steelhead, and landed two.

Those snippets of action were typical of that glorious 1980 season. Even in the seasons that followed, when there were not nearly as many fish, the Pocket remained the most dependable stretch of dry-fly water on the river. But then came the slide on Deer Creek and the great flow of silt into the North Fork, and the Pocket became one of the first casualties; silt filled in the slot at the head of the run and piled up in drifts behind the boulder that had allowed the Pocket to form. Where once there had been a hole eight feet deep at low water, there was scarcely two feet of depth at high water. For all practical purposes, the Pocket was gone—and with it the best steelhead dry-fly fishing I have ever known.

But even though the best seasons and the best water on the North Fork are both things of the past, I have continued in recent years to fish the dry fly as much as possible when water conditions have permitted. For this I am still rewarded with occasional moments of success, but it also has become necessary to develop a full measure of patience to deal with those increasingly long periods between successes, when the river seems altogether empty of fish in the pools and riffles below Deer Creek.

I remember one frustrating time when I went a full seven days without a single rise, growing quietly more desperate as I fished a little harder and a little longer each day in a futile effort to find a willing fish. Late on the last day before I had to return to the city I was fishing the lower end of the Stump Pool, still without success, when another angler approached from downstream and stood on the bank to watch me.

For a while he watched in silence. Then he said, "I see you're using a dry fly."

"Yes," I replied. "I use one whenever I can. In fact, that's all I've used for the past week. And I haven't risen a single fish." Sensing a willing listener, or perhaps merely anxious to vent a week's worth of fishing frustrations, I described in detail my seven days of angling futility while the stranger listened politely and made commiserating sounds at appropriate points in the monologue.

I had continued fishing while I spoke and both of us had kept a watchful eye on my riffle-hitched fly. I made another cast and the fly swung around below me, plowing its faithful little furrow in the current, then suddenly collided with a floating leaf and hooked it. Grunting in disgust, I gave the rod a flip; the fly came free and landed about three feet upstream. Suddenly there was a great wave behind it as a steelhead rose—and missed.

"Did you see that?" I shouted.

"Yes! Get your fly over him again. Maybe he'll come back!"

My fly was over the spot before the stranger even finished speaking. But the steelhead did not come back. I cast again and again, but nothing happened. I tried flipping the fly as I had before to get it away from the leaf, but that didn't help either. I changed flies and tried patterns that were lighter and darker, larger and smaller, but there was no response.

The other angler had stayed to watch it all. Finally he spoke again: "To fish all week without a rise, then hang your fly on a leaf, flip it off, and have a fish rise to it and miss—man, I don't believe it. You must be snakebit." With that he left me, as if fearful that some of my luck might rub off on him.

And he was right: For that week, at least, I was snakebit. I returned to the city with only the memory of that single fateful rise to mark eight long days of fishing.

Unfortunately, such fishless days are now more often the rule than the exception on the North Fork. But despite the hard times following the 1980 season—hard times that grew much worse during the years of the Deer Creek slide—the river had one more big surprise in store for me. It came on the Fourth of July, 1987.

I had just returned from a trip out of state and was delighted to find the Deer Creek slide apparently had stabilized and the North Fork was flowing clearly for the first time in three years. I spent joyful moments rediscovering parts of the riverscape that had remained hidden from view during all those years of silt and turbidity, and there was equal pleasure in seeing for the first time what changes the river had wrought for itself in that period. Best of all was the satisfaction of being able to fish my home river once again.

I quickly determined that the Pocket was still choked with silt and wrote it off as a lost cause, but the Elbow Hole had both lengthened and deepened during the unfishable years, so I started in there instead. Neither the Elbow nor the stretch below it yielded anything, however, and I still had seen no sign of fish when I came to the familiar slick at the head of the Stump Pool. I paused there and put on a fresh fly, secured with the usual riffle hitch, then resumed casting. The high-floating riffle-hitched fly left a trail as visible as a bright streak of chalk on a blackboard as it swung across the smooth surface of the slick.

Three casts brought nothing, but the fourth was greeted by a great bulge and a splash at the fly. Automatically reverting to my trout-fishing habits, I lifted the rod to set the hook instead of slacking off and giving the fish a chance to hook itself; as a consequence I missed the strike and the fly popped back to the surface and continued on its swing. Angry at myself, I resumed casting over the same spot, but a half-dozen offers of the same fly failed to produce another response, so I clipped it off and replaced it with a lighter-colored pattern.

After another half-dozen casts the steelhead rose again, this time quietly, sipping in the fly with hardly a visible disturbance in the current. This time I remembered to lower the rod and give slack, the line came tight, and in a moment I felt the weight of the fish.

I set the hook then, just to make sure, and started wading toward the beach, holding the rod high and ready for anything. But the steelhead was slow to make a move; it merely stayed where it was, holding deeply in the current where it had sucked in the fly, shaking itself once or twice in an effort to rid itself of the annoyance in its jaw. That was all.

I began trying to move it, to get it going so it would tire itself, but it simply stayed put and refused to yield to the pressure of the rod. That worried me; I sensed it was a heavy fish and I did not like the way it was behaving. I also had a hunch that it was going to be a while before the issue was decided.

And so it was. On its own initiative the fish finally came up and wallowed at the surface; I couldn't see it well, but it seemed to displace a lot of water. Then it turned and started downstream on a long run that quickly had me running in pursuit. At the end of the run the fish erupted from the water in a mighty leap, a yard-long length of writhing silver muscle, and I was shocked to see its size. It fell back with a huge splash and ran again, several times, with each run leading me farther downstream in obedient pursuit. Then came a second spectacular leap followed by a series of short, headlong rushes, until at last I found myself with a tired fish on a short line near the tail-out of a long, slow pool several hundred yards downstream from the slick where I had first hooked it.

Several times I led the fish toward the shallows, but each time it used its heavy weight and remaining strength to struggle back into deeper water—until the time finally came when it could do so no longer. Putting on as much strain as the six-pound test tippet could possibly absorb, I guided the weary fish to my hand and lifted it gently to the beach. It was a great buck steelhead, silver-bright except for a pale blush of rose just blooming on its sides, thick and fat from three years of rich ocean feeding. I placed my rod alongside and measured its length at a fraction over thirty-six inches and guessed its weight at between fifteen and sixteen pounds—by far the largest fish of any kind I had ever taken on a dry fly.

I removed the hook from its mouth and lifted the great fish gently back into the river, cradling it in the shallow water and moving it back and forth a long time until a normal pattern of respiration was restored. Finally I let it go and watched as it slowly blended with the current and became lost again in the river. But its memory will never be lost with me.

In recent seasons I have begun using the dry fly more and more often on other rivers—the Sauk, the Wenatchee, and the Elwha, just to name a few—and one of these offered an unusual oppor-

tunity to make some interesting observations about the way steelhead respond to flies, both wet and dry. Exercising the angler's favorite prerogative, I shall choose not to name the stream where these observations took place. Suffice it to say it is a small river that hosts a fine run of summer steelhead and has unusually clear water that often makes it possible to see the fish. One day while fishing this stream I came upon a school of about twenty steelhead lying plainly visible in a long crescent-shaped pool.

The wind was calm and the light was strong enough to see them well and I found a good vantage point upstream from which I could not only see the fish but reach them with a long cast.

At first I was content merely to watch and take notes on what I saw. The fish seemed restless, as if they sensed they were vulnerable to observation, and they moved collectively up the pool, then dropped downstream again, while individuals shifted station within the group. Their behavior did not appear to be hierarchical; that is, there did not appear to be any "lead fish," but rather some sort of collective will that determined the course followed by the whole group, rather like a flight of sandpipers turning in unison. There also were a few individuals that remained apart from the rest of the school, joining it briefly when it suited them, only to split off again and go their own ways.

A fisherman can stand the sight of a big school of steelhead only so long before he is compelled to fish for them, and it wasn't long before it occurred to me that the circumstances offered a perfect chance to make some comparisons in the way fish respond to different fly patterns. So I rigged up first with a sinking-tip line and began drifting various wet patterns through the school to see what the reaction would be.

The reactions were interesting, to say the least. The first cast with a hot-orange dressing drew instant attention from the fish; several turned and followed the fly closely for some distance, although non actually took it. A second pass with the same fly drew far less attention; a few fish shifted around nervously, but none turned toward or followed the fly. A third cast was greeted with almost total indifference.

The same pattern was repeated with other wet flies, both bright and dull; the first cast always seemed to provoke intense interest, the second much less, and the third no reaction at all. An exception came when I tied on a Skunk, a well-known Northwest pattern with black body and white wing; when the steelhead saw this fly coming they reacted with outright terror and the school broke up as fish fled in all directions. This curious response seemed most ironic since I always had found the Skunk to be a highly effective and reliable pattern; perhaps, among these fish, its reputation somehow had preceded it.

It took a long time for the pool to settle down again and for most of the steelhead to return to their places. As I waited I changed over to a floating line, and by the time things had returned more or less to normal I was ready to see how the fish would respond to a dry fly.

I started with a high-floating deer-hair pattern, fishing it with long slack-line downstream casts, then feeding more slack so the fly would float over the fish in a traditional drag-free float. The gentle current carried the fly repeatedly over the resting steelhead where they could see it easily, but none made a move toward it. After several tries brought no response, I added a riffle hitch and began skating the fly over the fish. On the first cast several steelhead reacted nervously and a couple even made half-hearted efforts to follow the fly, but quickly broke off the pursuit and returned to their stations. When several more casts failed to provoke a rise, I clipped off the big deer-hair pattern and replaced it with a smaller one, also riffle-hitched.

This combination immediately brought a much different reaction, and over the next hour I rose at least a dozen steelhead to the smaller skated pattern. In each case I could clearly see the steelhead catch sight of the fly, move to chase or intercept it, then break the surface with its snout right up against the fly. But I could also see that in nearly every instance the rising fish made no actual attempt to take the fly, being content merely to bump it instead. There were two exceptions, one of which I reacted to badly and missed, the other I hooked firmly—but ended up breaking the four-pound test leader that I had thought necessary to use in the exceptionally clear water.

Eventually the sun dipped behind the hills and threw long shadows over the pool and its school of steelhead, ending my observations and experiments for the day. But what I had seen, combined with earlier observations on other rivers, prompted some tentative conclusions.

One is that the novelty of a wet fly apparently wears off quickly on steelhead, and if no take is forthcoming on the first or second cast, then very likely there will be no take at all. This means that wet-fly fishermen will have a far better chance if they keep moving and cover as much water as they can instead of staying in one spot and continuing to fish the same water over and over again with the same fly (which always has seemed to me a foolish practice anyway). An exception would be the case in which a fish has been located and the angler continues to change flies in an effort to move it.

Conversely, the steelhead I observed never seemed to grow tired or wary of a riffle-hatched dry fly; over an hour's time I succeeded in raising a majority of the fish in the pool to such a fly. It's true that most of these seemed to be playful rises and the fish made few actual attempts to take the fly into their mouths, but that jibes with observations on other rivers that such playful rises are common and only in the minority of instances does a fish actually try to take the fly. The key point is that the fish never spooked and always seemed to retain an interest in the riffle-hitched patterns, and this would support the view that it *does* make sense for a dry-fly fisherman to cover the same water repeatedly with the same riffle-hitched dry fly.

Of course the only definitive thing about these conclusions is that this particular group of steelhead behaved in this particular way under the specific circumstances existing at the time on this specific stream, and it would be foolish to suggest that all steelhead would react the same way under all circumstances on every river. But the fact that these results do seem in accordance with the observed behavior of other fish in other rivers, at least in my experience, does seem to lend some credence to them.

Yet even the best observations and experiments shed little light on the basic question of why steelhead rise to a floating fly in the first place. Consider that these fish have returned to the river after being out in the ocean for one or two years or more, feeding on such things as herring, squid, and shrimp, foraging always beneath the surface, a thousand miles or more from the nearest hatching mayfly or caddis. So what possible motive could they have for rising through three or four feet of fast water to take a skated dry fly that resembles nothing they have seen since they were smolts?

It's interesting and fun to speculate on the answer to that question. We know, of course, that some steelhead do continue feeding on their upstream migrations, and quite likely their rise to a dry fly is a feeding response. But feeding behavior seems confined to a minority of fish and is rarely consistent, so it probably does not account for a high percentage of rises. It also doesn't explain why steelhead seem to respond more readily to a riffle-hitched fly behaving unnaturally than to a fly fished in the natural manner with a drag-free float.

Feeding behavior also is obviously not the reason for the steelhead's confounding habit of rising playfully to bump or splash at a riffle-hitched dry fly without actually trying to take it. Or perhaps this is more of an aggressive response than a playful one.

It seems unlikely that we shall ever know exactly why steelhead rise to a floating fly, and maybe that is the way it should be. Perhaps we should be content merely to know that they do rise, for whatever reason, and simply be glad for the fact and all that it means to our fishing.

Besides the dry fly there are many other steelhead fly-fishing methods to explore. Some angers have reported intriguing results fishing a tiny upstream weighted nymph, and others have enjoyed consistent success fishing large stonefly nymph imitations. Still others have experimented successfully with customized sinking-tip lines of varying lengths and densities and other innovative techniques.

I am certain all of these tactics hold a great deal of promise, but I do not think I could ever gain a full measure of satisfaction from any method that does not include the sight of a steelhead's mad rush to a floating fly. For me, that is the greatest moment in angling; nothing else comes close. The wet fly, weighted nymph, or some other subsurface method may yet prove to be the most effective means for taking fish, but I will always be content to fish on top and take pleasure from the fact that the steelhead also rises.

# 9 | On the
# Wenatchee

Early in autumn, when the limbs of the valley orchards are just beginning to grow heavy with the weight of ripening apples, the steelhead, migrant workers and fishermen all return to the Wenatchee River.

The steelhead come in obedience to ancient instinct, and theirs is by far the most difficult journey—for they must ascend a river that is no longer a river, the once-mighty Columbia reduced by a succession of stairstep dams to an emasculated chain of stagnant lakes. Designed by nature to oppose the heavy rush of water from the hills, to battle their way upstream through swift riffles and strong rapids, the steelhead must now instead try to

find and follow the faint trace of the river's dying pulse through a seemingly interminable series of quiet pools. At the head of each pool they also must face another of the concrete monoliths that block their ancient migratory route; there, in the maelstrom below the dam, they must find a small flow that marks the entrance to the fish ladder that offers them their only hope of passage and make their wearying way up the long stairstepped series of unnatural pools to continue their dangerous upstream journey.

Not once but seven times they must make this passage, and in all but one case after having made it they must again seek out the faint remnant of the river's current and follow it through miles of dead, warm, quiet water until they reach the next dam. The only exception is above McNary Dam, where the steelhead finally break out of the dam's sluggish backwater and into the open water of the Hanford Reach, the last free-flowing stretch of the Columbia. There, and only there, the river still sings its native song, still breaks swiftly over gravel bars and spills its way down broken, wrinkled runs; there, and only there, it still has energy and life, strength and movement. There, too, it is free of the Indian nets that bar the way through the quiet pools downstream and claim the lives of many, sometimes most, of the upstream steelhead. Yet even there, in the last threatened surviving stretch of river, the rise and fall of the current is subject to the manipulative whims of the masters of the dams, so even there the river is not truly free.

If somehow they escape all the perils of this upstream journey and survive the hurdle of the seventh dam, the remaining steelhead—much fewer in number now than when they entered the Columbia—soon feel the influence of a river that *is* still almost wholly free, a great rushing ribbon of cold clear water flowing down from the pine-clad eastern slopes of the Cascades. The Indians called it the *Wenatchi*, after a Yakima word meaning "river flowing from the canyon," and now on the white man's maps it is called the Wenatchee.

But the steelhead call it home. Drawn by its strength and coolness and remembered scent, they turn eagerly into it, perhaps sensing that their long and difficult journey at last is nearly at an end.

When the first steelhead arrive, the migrant workers cannot be far behind. They come not in obedience to instinct but in hopes of finding a share of the work that must be done in the orchards and packing houses when the apples grow ripe and heavy in the early fall. And although their journey is not as difficult as the upstream migration of the steelhead, it is by no means an easy one; many must travel an equal or perhaps even greater distance, coming from the fertile valleys of California or the Southwest, riding on cramped and smelly buses or in old cars of uncertain vintage, often with little more than the dirty clothing on their backs. In years when the harvest is good they all may find work, but more often it seems there is not enough work to go around; then only the lucky ones find temporary jobs and poor housing or shacks to live in, while those who are unlucky curl up to sleep in cars or in culverts or sometimes out in the orchards, under the stars, waiting and hoping improbably that some work will yet turn up—or perhaps not knowing where else they might go.

As September blends softly into October and the scent of ripe apples fills the warm Wenatchee valley afternoons, the fishermen also begin to arrive. Their journeys are short and easy and they travel in comfort, bent on pleasure, drawn by rumors of the presence of steelhead.

It has not always been so. Not so very many years ago the Wenatchee was nearly empty of steelhead, the victim of a chain of unhappy circumstances set in motion long ago by the construction of the first of the Columbia River dams. This was Rock Island Dam, started in 1933 just below the mouth of the Wenatchee, and its construction was begun with little knowledge or concern for the possible impacts on migratory runs of fish—an attitude that continued in effect for nearly forty years, contributing eventually to the decimation of native steelhead runs in the Wenatchee and virtually all other upper Columbia River tributaries.

No one knows the historic size of the Wenatchee's native run, for it was one of the first to suffer the effects of the dams. In 1938 Grand Coulee Dam shut off the Columbia River above the Wenatchee; too high to permit construction of a fish passage, the new dam in one stroke closed off upstream access to thousands of miles of the most productive salmon and steelhead spawning water in the world. In an effort to salvage some of the fish that otherwise would have reached those spawning tributaries, traps were set at Rock Island Dam to take as many returning fish as possible. These were transported to a new hatchery at Leavenworth on the Wenatchee River, or released to spawn in the river itself or one of its tributaries. Many did so, instantly compromising the genetic integrity of the river's native populations, built up over thousands of years of evolution. Even so, healthy runs of steelhead and salmon continued to return to the Wenatchee for the next twenty-five years, although the numbers of returning fish never quite equaled expectations and the Leavenworth hatchery never was able to reach its full capacity.

Meanwhile, more and more dams were going up on the Columbia, though nobody knew much more about their effect on steelhead and salmon than they had known when the first was built in 1933; as long as some fish were able to return, nobody seemed to care very much.

But in the late 1960s, numbers of adult fish returning to the Wenatchee and other upriver Columbia tributaries suddenly began dropping precipitously. Always before, biologists had estimated that 5 to 6 percent of the steelhead smolts produced by these rivers would return as adults, and this pattern seemed to hold true as late as 1966; but by 1969 the ratio had fallen to 2.5 percent, by 1972 it was down to 1 percent, and a year later the number of returning adults equaled only a tiny fraction of 1 percent of the number of smolts that years before had set out for the sea.

By 1975 the count of steelhead ascending the fish ladder at Bonneville Dam, the first obstruction in their path, had declined to only eighty-five thousand—only that many fish for all the vast sprawling reach of the Columbia River Basin and its uncounted number of upstream tributaries with their thousands of miles of water reaching all the way to the foot of the Rockies; only that many for the White Salmon and the Wind, for the Klickitat and the Deschutes and the John Day, for the Snake and the Clearwater and the Grande Ronde and the Imnaha, for the Yakima and the Wenatchee and the Methow and the Okanogan, and for a host of lesser rivers. The salmon runs had declined to a similar ebb.

When the scope of the disaster became apparent, growing public alarm prompted some long-overdue studies of the problem—and at long last the fatal effects of the dams began to be revealed and understood. Biologists found that eighty to ninety percent of the outmigrating steelhead and salmon smolts were being chopped to pieces in the blades of hydroelectric turbines or killed

by nitrogen supersaturation in the turbulence below the spill-
ways, a cruel phenomenon like the "bends" in human divers that
causes bubbles to form in a fish's blood or rise under its skin or
burst inside its eyes.

The problem of the turbines had not been apparent in the early
years of dam construction because the smolts' migration always
had taken place in spring when the water was high enough that
most of it could be spilled over the dams and fish would not be
sucked through the turbines. But the proliferation of dams had
produced a great surplus of electricity that was being sold at fire-
sale prices, and this in turn had attracted industries such as aluminum smelters with huge appetites for energy. As more and
more of these energy-intensive industries went on line, they
gradually used up the generating capacity of the river so that even
during the high spring runoff there was no spare water left to spill
over the dams; all of it was routed through the turbines instead,
and the downstream smolts were swept along with it to a violent
death.

The threat of nitrogen supersaturation also had been slow to
appear, but as more and more dams were built—each one adding
to the problem—the cumulative effect eventually reached fatal
proportions, killing many of the fish that somehow survived the
nightmarish passage through the turbines.

Nor was that all. The expanding number of warm slack-water
lakes behind the dams created artificial habitats in which scrap
fish and predators flourished, and these also were beginning to
take a rising toll of the relatively few smolts that managed to
escape death in the turbines or from nitrogen supersaturation.
For young fish the path downstream to the sea had become a fatal
gantlet nearly impossible to pass.

The Wenatchee River steelhead run was among those most
dramatically affected by these problems; by the mid-1970s it had
been reduced to only a few hundred fish, perhaps only a few
score, and was close to the point of extinction. And extinction
likely would have been its eventual fate, along with many other

steelhead and salmon runs, had public outrage not forced a series of remedial measures.

The Army Corps of Engineers, the agency most responsible for creating the problems, bowed to pressure from the public and from other government agencies and resumed spilling water over the dams during the spring migration period. When that was not possible, the Corps set up fish screens to trap migrating smolts, then hauled them downstream in hatchery trucks and barges for eventual release below the dams. The Corps also began fitting dams with devices known as "flip lips," designed to minimize nitrogen supersaturation.

These desperate measures staved off extinction of the runs, but they still left the Columbia and Snake rivers and their tributaries with only token remnants of their former native populations—and most of those remnants were fish raised in hatcheries and trucked to the sea in a sad imitation of the natural life cycle of wild steelhead and salmon.

Out of this disastrous shambles of mismanagement, and after seasons of bitter and sometimes acrimonious debate, Congress sought to bring order by finally approving legislation creating the Northwest Regional Power Council. To this agency it gave the formidable task of bringing some sort of intelligent direction to the great network of hydroelectric dams built by the Bonneville Power Administration and a host of public and private Northwest utilities, and the even greater task of trying to restore the fish and wildlife populations the dams had destroyed.

The latter part of this mandate might easily have been ignored—certainly there was pressure enough from utility and industry lobbyists to ignore it—but fortunately the first appointed members of the new Power Council took it seriously. They ordered a study of the status of fish and wildlife populations in the Columbia River Basin and used the findings as the basis for an aggressive program to restore both populations and habitats.

The program included a new set of rules for utility managers. For the first time they were required to consider the needs of fish along with those of power-gobbling industries. This meant that, like it or not, they would have to spill water over the dams during spring runoff to assure the safe downstream passage of outmigrating smolts, no matter what the demands of the aluminum smelters. It was a bitter pill for the utility bureaucrats and their bed partners in the aluminum industry to swallow, but they had no choice.

The effects of these and other positive steps were almost immediate, and adult salmon and steelhead began to return to the upper Columbia tributaries in greater numbers than had been seen for a decade. The Wenatchee River steelhead were among those benefiting from these measures, and by the early 1980s anglers who had fished the river through its lean years were beginning to whisper to their friends that the Wenatchee run was back. As word spread, state authorities, in a wise effort to protect what had been restored at such great cost, imposed catch-and-release regulations on the river, instantly turning it into a Mecca for fly fishers from all over the Northwest.

So now, each year in the early fall the steelhead and the fishermen once again return to the Wenatchee along with the migrant workers. But only the fishermen are at full liberty to enjoy the riches of the river and the season, and those riches are abundant—for the Wenatchee is certainly one of the most beautiful rivers on earth.

For one who travels to it from the coastal cities, as I do, it is especially appealing. The highway through the Cascades comes upon it suddenly and without warning, just where the river breaks out of the forest and into the head of Tumwater Canyon and begins its eastward plunge toward the Columbia. It is already a full-blown river at this point, clear and bright and strong, and the canyon it enters is narrow, with steep weathered rock walls furrowed by ledges and terraces to which pines, firs, broadleaf maples and quaking aspens precariously cling. By early October, when the fishing starts to peak, the hillsides bleed with spectacular color, as if each individual dying leaf were lit by some bright internal flame, and the explosion of colors offers a breathtaking contrast to the translucent foam-flecked emerald surface of the river.

The little mountain town of Leavenworth lies within the folds of a great S-shaped turn of the river at the lower end of Tumwater Canyon, and there the river gathers in the flow of its main tributary, the Icicle, coming from the south. Below Leavenworth the country changes abruptly, the pine-clad slopes giving way to a broad valley framed with brown and yellow hills covered sparsely with dry bunch grass and patches of crimson sumac. The valley

bottom is filled with orchards, occupying nearly every foot of fertile ground, the trees all drawn up in neat, well-ordered ranks like regiments standing rigidly at attention. Spaced among the orchards is a series of small towns strung out along the river like beads on a chain—Peshastin, Dryden, Cashmere, Monitor, and finally the city of Wenatchee itself, at the end of the chain near the river's mouth.

Here, in these last fifteen miles of its rush toward the dead water of the Columbia, the river has a broad channel and plenty of room to move around in, yet it still flows swiftly with all the energy and strength gained in its long fall through the upstream canyon. It forms broad runs and noisy riffles, breaks into long choppy stretches of pocket water, and pauses briefly in complicated eddies and complex pools. And here the fishermen gather to intercept returning steelhead.

The restored Wenatchee River steelhead run reached its peak in 1983 and the fishing that year was incredible. One September morning I made the long drive over from Seattle and parked my truck in a dusty turnaround near the old Lower Monitor Bridge, then waded out to fish the run beneath the bridge. There I found an old friend, Buzz Fiorini, who was just leaving the water after releasing a small steelhead; he was full of excited talk about the number of fish in the river. A platoon of bait fishermen had taken up station on the rocky bank across the river, lobbing short casts into the deepest part of the run—bait fishing was still legal, despite the catch-and-release regulation—but after Buzz left I had the water on my side of the river to myself.

The wading, as usual, was tricky, and it was necessary to go in waist-deep or even deeper to get within casting distance of the best water. Even then it took a long double-hauled cast to drop my riffle-hitched dry fly over the water where I suspected fish would be, and the play of the swift current on the long line made the fly difficult to control. It also made it nearly impossible to set the hook in a rising fish, as I soon learned, for two steelhead quickly came up in spectacular splashing rises and I missed them both, feeling only a brief pull from one and nothing at all from the other.

It took three-quarters of an hour to fish through the run. While I did so the bait fishermen on the other side of the river wrestled four steelhead to the beach and let them go. But then the run went dead; I fished through it a second time without a touch, and the bait fishermen also seemed to have run out of action.

So after that I left the drift and went on down to fish the County Park Run, a great sweep of water that skirts the edge of a neat and well-manicured public park and campground, a stretch more than a quarter of a mile long where there is nearly always room to fish even when the river is crowded, as it was on this day. Two other fishermen already were in the drift, but both were well down, so I started in at the head. On my third cast a steelhead came up in a perfect head-and-tail rise to take the fly and was hooked firmly. It jumped only once but fought stubbornly in the fast water, twice taking the line down to the backing before it finally surrendered and allowed itself to be steered into quiet water where I could twist the fly free and let it go. It was a hen steelhead of about seven pounds, stoutly built and lightly bronzed as if it had been sunburned during its long upriver passage, far different in appearance from the sleek silvery steelhead of the short-run coastal rivers.

I fished a total of three hours that day, caught one steelhead, missed two, and saw seven others landed—a good indication of the abundance of fish in the river. There have been other good days, but none other I can remember when there seemed to be so many fish around.

Over the years I have grown to know the lower river intimately and each season I look forward to the fall fishing there. The run beneath the Lower Monitor Bridge remains a favorite, and although it is no easier to fish now than it was in 1983, it is nearly always worth fishing. It is not the most esthetic place—the river there is full of construction rubble, dirty pigeons roost in recesses under the old concrete bridge deck, and the bridge supports are covered with spray-painted graffiti ("Please Write—Mother" is one of the few decipherable or socially acceptable messages)—but it is prime water, and if there are steelhead anywhere in the lower river they are likely to be found here.

The County Park Run is also always an interesting place to fish, not only because of the water and the promise of steelhead, but also because of the people who congregate there. It is a favorite place for the migratory workers to bathe—those who can't afford the twenty-five-cent showers in the park's public restroom do their washing in the river for free—and I have seen as many as eight of them in the river at a time, all lathered up and chattering in Spanish while a portable radio on the beach played Mexican music in incongruous counterpoint to the sounds of the river.

The county park also is a favorite stopping place for down-on-their-luck itinerants, who stop to wash or rest under the shade of the trees, or perhaps beg a handout from the local picnickers or fishermen. Each one has his own story, and some of the stories are touching. A battered van with Maryland license plates is the traveling home of a family that includes a wiry, curly-haired little man with tattoos on his arms, his black wife who says nothing and wears a bleak, hopeless expression, and their two little children who look bewildered. The husband tells a sad tale: One night out of Denver, with his wife and children asleep in the back of the van, he stopped to pick up a pair of hitchhikers, thinking their conversation might keep him awake for another hundred miles. Sometime during the ride one of the hitchhikers reached into his wife's purse and removed a billfold containing $385, a loss not discovered until long after the hitchhikers had been left behind. Although the man doesn't say so, there is an impression this was all the money the family had; now, the man says, he is looking for work in the orchards, hoping to make up for the loss.

A big blond potbellied man from California has a more upbeat story to tell. From his van he produces an enormous elk horn, half of what must have been a prodigious rack. He says he got it near West Yellowstone.

Road kill? I ask.

He nods and says he wishes he could have found the other half. He talks about sawing off the butt and making it into a belt buckle, then selling the rest. He asks about the steelhead fishing and says he hopes to stay a couple of months while the fish are in. He already has found work in an apple warehouse and says he prefers working the warehouses to picking in the orchards because it's always cooler inside the warehouses. But he looks as if he might be cut out for better things.

A railroad track runs along the river across from the county park and all day long the freights rumble back and forth on the Seattle-to-Chicago run, the cars leaning as they go around the curves so that you wonder if they are going to topple into the river. These days the trains consist mostly of long strings of flatcars carrying container vans, but sometimes there are still a few conventional boxcars sandwiched in among them, and occasionally a grimy gap-toothed hobo waves from an open boxcar door. The engineers usually wave, too, probably wishing they could be out wading the river instead of looking forward to several hundred more miles of monotonous track with shimmering waves of heat rising from the rails.

Between trains the railroad track is a main thoroughfare for a continuing procession of footbound itinerants, a sort of Oregon Trail for modern wanderers. Most carry backpacks and there is nothing much unusual about them, but occasionally there comes one who has fashioned a more imaginative way to carry his worldly goods. One pulls a triangular-shaped cart fashioned out of plastic pipe and a wheel off a baby carriage, a modern wheeled version of the ancient Indian travois. The pipes flex and the cart rises and falls rhythmically as it bounces over the railroad ties, and you wonder how many miles more it can go before it falls hopelessly apart.

The County Park Run also is a noisy place to fish. Big trucks roar past on the freeway on one side of the river and the freights grumble and squeak past on the other, and sometimes you can feel their ticklish vibration through the rocks on the river bottom. Crop-dusting helicopters fly over at treetop level, the beat of their blades against the thick valley air becoming audible long before they come into sight. The steady rushing sounds of the river try to compete with all this manmade industrial noise, but the manmade noise usually gains the upper hand. Still, it is not unpleasant fishing, for the coolness of the river is always a blessed relief from the afternoon heat, and the steeply rising hills beyond the railroad track bring to mind pleasant memories of New Zealand's South Island or the slopes around Idaho's Silver Creek. And of course there are always the fish.

The fish are splendid. Considering all the trials they must pass to reach this place, you are quite ready and willing to forgive them if they do not always fight as well as you think they should. But often they fight even better than you thought they could, and it seems altogether fitting that the regulations should require their release; it would be unfair, even tragic, to think of killing any fish that has come so far and endured so much. It is true they are no longer steelhead of the pure native blood that once coursed through the fish of this river, and they may not even be wild fish by strict definition of the term, but the mere fact that they are here, alive, seems nothing short of a miracle. They deserve to go on living.

That is true now more than ever. For since the magnificent 1983 run there has never been another quite as good, and over the past several seasons the number of fish returning to the Wenatchee has again dwindled sharply. One reason seems to be that the Wenatchee run is especially vulnerable to Indian gill nets in the slackwater pools of the Columbia far downstream and suffers disproportionately cruel and heavy losses compared with runs bound for other upstream tributaries. Another reason may be that increasing numbers of steelhead from all the rivers are being taken in vicious unregulated drift-net fisheries far at sea. Or perhaps the dams are beginning to exert yet another sinister, unrecognized effect on the steelhead.

But although they may be fewer in number, the steelhead still return faithfully to the Wenatchee every autumn, just as the apples are ripening and the migratory workers begin arriving to pick them. The fishermen are never far behind, and they start crowding the river about the time the first leaves begin falling like bright flares up in Tumwater Canyon. Itinerant panhandlers still pick their way along the railroad tracks next to the County Park Run, bound like the steelhead for some mysterious destination known only to themselves.

All these things are now a part of the Northwest steelhead tradition, and all of them are now a part of my life. Along with the steelhead and the migrant workers, I expect to return to the Wenatchee every autumn—for as many more autumns as I have.

# 10 | IN THE ESTUARIES

I FOLLOWED the little-traveled narrow road to the familiar metal gate with its imposing sign that warned all trespassers to stay away. The gate was unlocked as always, but its metal was cold to the touch on this winter morning, so cold my fingers stuck to it briefly as I swung the gate wide and groped for an old piece of wood that was used to prop it open. Then I drove the truck through and left it with the engine running while I got out to close the gate again.

The noise of the truck started the Widow's dogs barking and the racket brought her out to see who was calling. Her house was

just inside the gate and she shared it with an ever-changing menagerie of dogs, cats, horses, ducks, and chickens. Beyond the house a narrow pair of ruts led downhill through a pasture to a rocky point that guarded the entrance to a secluded saltwater bay with a lazy, fair-sized creek running in at its head. The bay absorbed the sluggish current so quickly and thoroughly that it was never quite possible to say exactly where the stream ended and the bay began; but that is nearly always the case in estuaries.

The place was well off the beaten path, a quiet backwater of Puget Sound where the tide came and went with diurnal preci-

sion, where herons and kingfishers and bobbing grebes all fished
and seals and sea lions sometimes joined them, where gulls
wheeled incessantly and cried their wailing cries, where cutthroat, salmon, and steelhead mingled in their appointed seasons. Surrounded by a boggy shoreline and mud flats laced with
spots of quicksand, the bay was nearly inaccessible except from
the rocky point below the Widow's place; fortunately, she had
granted access to me and a few of the other fishermen who peri-
odically found their way to her gate. In exchange for the privilege
of access she asked little, usually just the chance for some conversation to liven up her lonely days, or occasional help with
chores that her age prevented her from doing by herself.

I stopped the truck in front of her porch and got out to say
hello. She was wearing her usual morning frown, which eased
somewhat when she recognized me through thick glasses that
magnified her eyes. The stem on one side of her glasses was
broken off so that they rested unevenly on the bridge of her nose,
and the effect was to give her a slightly tilted look. Her teeth,
which she exposed when she talked, were the same color and
shape as the rows of old pilings out in the bay. But despite her
formidable appearance and matching raspy voice, she was friendly and seemed pleased to see me—as she always seemed pleased
to see any familiar face that posed no threat and might be someone she could engage in conversation for a while.

We stood there chatting while the smoke from her woodstove
rose in a pencil-thin column in the frozen air of the early winter
morning. As we talked, a fat puppy came bumbling up and em-
braced me with muddy paws. It was followed closely by a larger
companion of uncertain canine ancestry. Nearby was another
dog, a large dark animal with sharply pointed ears, a long slender
snout, and yellow wolflike eyes; it was tethered by a stout chain,
the only animal so restrained, and from its look I was glad to see
it wasn't free to roam. Cats of various sizes, shapes, and colors
lurked in the brush or peered out from behind the railing on the
Widow's deck. There was a commotion behind me and I turned
to see a pair of half-wild spotted hybrid chickens roosting well up

in the limbs of a big fir tree. I turned back just in time to witness a parade of ducks pass between me and the Widow on the porch, but she took no notice of them—nor, indeed, of any of the other birds and animals that brought movement to the landscape everywhere I looked. One might have thought Noah's ark had run aground on her beach.

It developed there were no chores she needed done that day, so I hurried through the conversational pleasantries, then got back in my truck and drove down through the pasture where a pair of scruffy-looking ponies kept the grass cropped short. The ponies were there as usual, their backs tinged silver with frost, their breath forming clots of steam in the cold morning.

The ruts leading down through the pasture ended just short of a great tangle of blackberries through which a path had been cut to the rocky beach where the tide lapped gently at the shore. Somewhere, out beneath that gently undulating tide, I hoped bright steelhead might be waiting. It was the heart of winter, but the weather had been dry for weeks and all the rivers were low, including the little creek at the head of the estuary; if any steelhead had come back from their long sea journeys to spawn in the creek, they should still be out in the estuary, waiting for the creek to rise enough to permit them to enter. That was the prospect that had drawn me here.

I parked the truck, removed the little aluminum pram from its perch atop the canopy, and began to rig up, still feeling a sense of relief that my encounter with the Widow had been brief. She was always anxious to talk because she had so few visitors and conversation was a luxury she was not often able to indulge; this I knew and so I always tried my best to oblige her, but I was always at least as anxious to go fishing as she was to talk, and it was difficult to maintain the patience necessary to preserve the conversational amenities.

The thought made me glance up the hill to see if she might be on her way down to renew the conversation, having forgotten something she intended to say. But I saw only ponies and ducks and dogs and cats and chickens.

That reminded me of the time I had come here to fish when the Widow was away from home. She had told me often to drive through whether she was home or not, so I had done so, parked my truck in the pasture, launched my boat, and gone fishing, glad for the opportunity to escape the obligatory conversation. But by the time I had returned, so had she, and when she saw me loading up my boat she came tramping down through the pasture.

"I don't care about myself," she said by way of opening the conversation, "but my animals are starving and I hate to see them suffer. Will you take me to town so I can buy some food?"

Slightly taken aback, I assured her I would be glad to do so. She turned and stomped up the hillside to get her purse from the house while I finished loading the truck, then drove up to meet her there.

We chatted idly on the five-mile trip to town, and when we got there I went into the store to help her shop and carry out her groceries, including a fifty-pound bag of dry dog food that I hefted into the back of the truck. When everything was loaded she went to the cashier's checkstand to pay the bill. She opened her purse, peered inside, then turned the purse upside down and shook it. Nothing fell out.

"Mercy me!" she rasped. "I seem to have left my checkbook at home. That won't do at all." She turned and glared at me. "I guess you'll have to put all that stuff back."

"Oh no, that's all right," I said quickly. "Let me pay for it."

"No! No! I wouldn't hear of it."

"It's all right, really. You've let me launch my boat at your place for years, and that's worth a lot to me. The least I can do is pay for your groceries."

She scowled and seemed to consider that. "Well, all right," she said finally. "But I'll write you a check and pay you back when we get home."

The store owner was standing behind the counter, tapping one foot impatiently while other shoppers formed in line behind us. He grabbed the twenty-dollar bill I gave him and quickly handed back the few cents due in change. I hustled the Widow outside and into the truck and started for her place. As soon as we got there she went inside the house while I fetched the groceries from the back of the truck and carried them into her kitchen.

The kitchen was an incredible place. The walls, cupboards, and counters all seemed alive and I counted eighteen different cats and seven different dogs before their comings and goings caused me to lose track. The oven door was open and two cats were curled up inside; other cats came and went through an open window. The stench was worse than a barnyard on a hot summer day.

I put the groceries on the counter while the Widow rummaged around the house, looking for her checkbook. "Where would a respectable white person hide her checkbook?" she muttered to herself as she looked first in the nooks and crannies of an old desk, then flipped through bound-up stacks of old letters and bills, then searched the freezing compartment of the refrigerator. I heard a ripping sound and turned to see several cats clustered around the grocery bags; they already had crawled inside one and torn open the wrapper on a loaf of bread, dragging out several slices that they then began to eat. I shooed them away and tied the tops of the grocery bags to keep them from getting in again.

By this time I had decided it would be worth a lot more than twenty dollars just to be able to leave, and I said as much to the Widow as politely as I could. But she insisted that I write down my address so that when she found her checkbook she could send me a check in the mail. I wrote it down quickly, then took my leave, breathing the clean outside air deeply and gratefully. And I didn't really expect I would ever see a check in the mail.

Which I didn't. But the next time I saw Alan Pratt, another of the fishermen who enjoyed launching privileges from the Widow, I told him the story.

"So she did that to you, too," was all he said.

When everything was ready I launched my little pram from the rocky shore, relieved to get away before the Widow might decide she wanted further words with me. Pushing off with one oar, I headed out into the estuary, rowing hard against the outgoing tide.

Going out into an estuary on a winter day is like stepping into a Matthew Brady photograph. There is no color and not much definition, only soft outlines in shades of sepia and gray: great, wide expanses of metallic gray sky, the dark shifting surface of the tide, the even darker silhouettes of wind-bent firs and cedars leaning from the slopes along the shore. An estuary in winter presents a scene that is nearly always easy on the eyes; there is nothing bright or startling to be seen—nothing, that is, unless one is lucky enough to hook a steelhead and have it jump suddenly, all bright and gleaming, into the dark day.

The tide was high at this hour of the morning, but the calendar promised a long all-day run-out culminating in a minus tide. I knew from past experience that if any steelhead were present it would be difficult to find them when the tide was high, so my plan was to fish for cutthroat in the morning and look for steelhead in the low water of the afternoon. I rowed to a spot where I had often found sea-run cutthroat in the past, dropped anchor, and began fishing. Before long I saw a quick rise, cast to it, and was immediately fast to a spunky thirteen-inch cutthroat. I released it and quickly hooked another, which just as quickly shook itself loose.

After that I went for a long time without seeing or hooking another fish. The tide continued to ebb all the while, gathering force and momentum until it was flowing like a river out through the narrow confines of the estuary. I slipped anchor then and let the pram ride with the tide, down past the Widow's point, past the oyster beds that lay beyond it, all the way down to the sand spit that marked the estuary's outer limits, and out into the open, unprotected water of the sound. Fortunately the day had remained calm and there was no threatening chop; except for scattered furious tidal rips, the water was glassy and still.

Still enough, in fact, that when a fish rose nearby I could easily see the spreading ring of water it had left. I cast toward the spot

and saw a big boil on the surface after the fly landed, but there was no answering pull when I lifted the rod to try to set the hook. Then I remembered I was still using the same small fly I had used for the cutthroat, so I clipped it off, replaced it quickly with a larger pattern, and resumed casting to the same area.

After a few casts, something grabbed the fly with forceful strength and a great wild steelhead exploded out of the water, its silver flanks bending and flapping and throwing spray high and far into the cold winter day. The fish began running almost before it was back in the water, and the battered old reel I use for salt-water fishing struggled to keep up with the sudden demand for line. Far out across the sandy tidal shallows the steelhead ran, turning its flanks to catch the flow of the outgoing tide and add extra momentum to its run. Then the fish leaped again, far away among the contending currents of an angry rip where frenzied gulls were plunging to feed on baitfish swept to the surface by the boiling tide. And this time, when the steelhead fell back to the water, the fly was no longer in its mouth.

Shaken by the violence of the brief encounter, I reeled in the long length of slack line and backing with trembling fingers, then checked to see if the fly was still attached. It was; the fish had simply shaken free. But I decided to clip off the fly anyway and tie it on again with a fresh knot.

After that came another long spell with no action, although I did see two more fish rise and judged from the size of the surface disturbances that both must have been steelhead. By this time it was midafternoon and there was only another hour and a half left in the short winter day, so reluctantly I hoisted the anchor and began the long, difficult row back against the tide, still rushing outward as if determined to drain the estuary dry.

By the time I arrived back off the Widow's point my arms and back were aching from the long pull. Already the light was fading from the metallic sky, and beyond the pasture, up at the top of the hill, I could see the lights going on in the Widow's house. The day-long ebb had emptied the estuary so that only a single large tidal pool remained off the point, and even there the water was so shallow that from time to time my boat grated on rocky bottom or oyster shell. A few more pulls on the oars and I would be back on the beach, ready to call it a day.

But then I noticed a quiet rise not far away, just a quick little dimple in the slick moving surface of the tide. The temptation was too much to resist, so I stood up wearily, false-cast a couple of times to work out the proper length of line, then dropped my fly over the spot and started a rapid retrieve. A ripple appeared behind the fly as if a torpedo were chasing it, and I accelerated the retrieve even more; the ripple kept pace and followed the fly halfway to the boat, then abruptly disappeared.

Excited now, I glanced around and saw another rise, then another, then the unmistakable sight of a broad gunmetal back creasing the surface as a big steelhead rolled. At least a dozen fish were in the pool, rising and rolling restlessly in the twilight.

During the next hour I hooked five steelhead. One was broken at the strike and another lost after just a momentary connection, but the others were landed after a succession of spectacular battles in which the fish behaved with a wild violence I had never experienced from any steelhead in fresh water. The smallest fish was a beautiful bright buck of about five and a half pounds, the next largest a slightly darker buck of about nine pounds, and the largest a lovely bright twelve-pound hen. The latter was the best fish of all, jumping seven times and running repeatedly far into the backing, threatening several times to foul the line on oyster shells that were just beginning to show their jagged tops above the still fast-ebbing tide.

It was pitch dark and the temperature had dipped below freezing by the time I finally quit fishing, but the hour-long rush of steelhead-induced adrenalin had kept me from even noticing the cold. The adrenalin wore off quickly, however, and by the time I had loaded up my boat and put away my gear, I was shivering and tired—but my mind was still full of the warm, glowing memory of all that had happened. I even felt up to facing the Widow again on my way out.

It was quite by accident that I first discovered the possibilities of fishing for winter steelhead in estuaries. The discovery came one early March day when Ed Foss and I set out to explore for sea-run cutthroat in the southern reaches of Puget Sound. In those days Ed and I spent a lot of time together searching for sea-runs, and on this occasion we had selected an area new to us both. It looked promising on the map, which showed four large creeks flowing into a saltwater channel at roughly equal intervals about a quarter of a mile apart. According to the map there were no roads along the channel shore, which meant the creekmouths probably were accessible only by water and therefore likely to be only lightly fished.

A road did swing out to touch the channel's shore about a half-mile south of the spot where the first creek showed on the map, and we followed it until we found a place to launch our boats. The day was cool and bright with a few fluffy cumulus clouds off in the distance but no hint of rain; in fact, it had been an unseasonably dry winter, with little rain or snow for weeks.

We cranked up our small outboards and made the half-mile run northward through open water with a light chop, paralleling the shoreline until up ahead we could see an opening in the rocky beach and the line of trees beyond it. The opening marked the mouth of the first creek, just where the map had said it would be, and the creek had carved out a nice little protected bay for itself in the edge of the channel. But the map was out of date in one very important respect: The bay had a road around it and was half-rimmed with summer homes and cabins, many with floats or docks in front and boats riding at anchor. That was a disappointment; it meant the bay was anything but lightly fished. But as long as we were there we decided to try it anyway, and I made a few casts and saw a couple of schools of sea perch and some candlefish but no cutthroat before I decided I didn't like the vibrations I was getting from the place. So I started the outboard again and headed back out into the channel, leaving Ed behind to explore the bay at greater length.

I headed north again, still paralleling the channel shore, looking for another opening that would mark the entry of the second creek. The ground along the shoreline rose steeply until I was motoring along the foot of a high clay and sandstone cliff with only a narrow stretch of beach at the bottom and scattered treetops barely visible at the top. The cliff extended northward without a break as far as I could see, and I began to wonder where the second creek could be.

Then suddenly I came upon a narrow opening in the face of the cliff, a doorlike passage completely hidden until one was directly in its front. It was scarcely twenty feet wide and the tide was flowing out of it strongly, so strongly that when I turned into the opening the little outboard had to strain at top throttle to make headway. When the boat finally cleared the narrow funnellike opening, I shut off the motor, drifted into quiet water, and stopped to take a look around. I was inside an amazing little secret bay, several hundred yards long and perhaps 150 yards wide, surrounded by steep cliffs except at its most inland point, where a good-sized creek plunged out of a narrow passage through the woods. With the single glaring exception of a large sailboat that somehow had worked its way through the narrow passage and now rode quietly at anchor in the center of the bay, there was no sign of human settlement.

The sailboat appeared deserted, but so at first did the bay as I began to methodically explore the shallow water along its shoreline, looking for cutthroat. Then I heard a splash out in deeper water and turned just in time to see what appeared to be a giant steelhead vault clear of the surface. I rowed quickly to the spot, looked down through the clear water and saw something that took my breath away: A great school of steelhead—fifty of them; no, a hundred; no, perhaps as many as two hundred—was cruising slowly around the little bay in what seemed to be a broad circle. Some of the fish were dark and obviously had been there quite a while, waiting for rain to raise the level of the creek at the head of the bay, but others were still mint-bright and I could see the light glinting from their sides as they passed.

Scarcely believing my eyes, I cast ahead of the school and let my fly sink down as the lead fish approached. When they got close I started a quick retrieve; a big old buck saw the fly and peeled off from the formation to follow, and I watched with rising excitement as it caught up, opened its mouth, and closed it on the fly. But in my excitement I struck too quickly, before the fish could turn, and there was only a brief moment of contact before the fly came free; through the clear water I saw the fish shake its head a time or two, then turn slowly back to rejoin the others in the school.

Hurriedly, I cast again. Another buck turned, followed, and took the fly. This time I waited until the fish turned away, then hauled back on the rod and set the hook firmly. The fish responded instantly with a long run across the bay and I had to clamp down hard on the reel to turn it short of the sailboat's mooring line; it was a near thing, but the fish slowly came around in a wide turn that carried it away from the threat.

The turn also narrowed the distance between us so that I was able to regain some line, but then the fish ran again, taking even more line and backing than before. Two or three more times it did this and the struggle went on in such fashion for nearly ten minutes before the steelhead began to show signs of tiring. Eventually I wrestled it in close to the boat and was beginning to think about how I was going to land it when the fish turned suddenly and ran again, this time directly toward the shore. An old tree limb lay there, partly submerged in the shallow water, and the fish ran under it and stirred up a cloud of mud on the far side. For a moment I felt the terrible vibration of the line rubbing on the waterlogged limb; then the leader broke. I swore out loud and an echo from the surrounding cliffs underscored the obscenity, as if the cliffs were disappointed too. The steelhead, now free, swam wearily back toward its companions in the deeper water while I retrieved the line with its broken leader.

By the time I had repaired the leader and replaced the fly, Ed had joined me, having also found the narrow entrance to this hidden little Shangri-la of a bay. I told him about the steelhead and he quickly took up a position across the bay where he could intercept the cruising formation of fish, visible now as a great dark mass moving through the water. Within moments he was into a bright steelhead of about six pounds, which put up a vigorous fight before he landed it. It was quickly followed by another, a twin of the first both in size and in the way it fought.

Meanwhile, I had caught a pair of sea-run cutthroat that seemed to materialize out of nowhere to seize my fly before a steelhead could reach it, perhaps the only time in my life I have been unhappy about catching cutthroat. It was true we had set out in hopes of finding sea-runs, but now that we had also found steelhead I was interested in them only.

We fished on and the steelhead responded with several more

follows but no takes. By this time the tide had changed and was flooding quickly back through the narrow entrance to the bay, and the steelhead seemed to become less active and far more difficult to see as the water level rose around us. When the fish no longer seemed willing to respond to a wet fly, I switched over to a big floating pattern, skated on the surface; this seemed to make them nervous, but none actually came up to take the fly. Then the water became too deep to see the fish at all, and although we continued casting blindly and eventually moved up toward the creek mouth in hopes the steelhead might have done likewise, it was as if they had vanished into thin air. And then it was time for us to go.

Ed was happy with having taken a pair of wild fish, and although my own score was only one fish stung and another lost, I was pleased and excited about the discoveries we had made. Never before had I seriously considered the possibilities of catching winter steelhead in the hundreds of small estuaries around the rim of Puget Sound, but now that I had seen for myself that such opportunities existed I was anxious to explore other places where steelhead might be found and experiment with techniques for taking them.

Which I soon did. But I also soon discovered that the right conditions for taking steelhead in the estuaries don't come along very often. Most important is a prolonged spell of dry weather, preferably in January, enough to lower the creeks flowing into the estuaries so that the returning steelhead must wait for them to rise. Dry spells come infrequently on Puget Sound at any time of year, but especially in January, and my diary tells me that in the fifteen years since Ed and I first found steelhead in that little hidden harbor, there have been only two other dry spells long enough to result in good estuary fishing. More often the winter months bring day after day of steady rain so that the creeks are always brim full and the steelhead hardly need pause as they move through the estuaries and head upstream.

Besides dry weather and low water, another requirement for good estuary fishing is a steady succession of low afternoon tides, the lower the better. It took some time for me to catch on to this, for conventional wisdom is that estuary fishing is always best during high tide. Certainly there is no doubt that high tide is the best time to fish for the coho salmon that return to many estuaries in the fall; the salmon seem to press forward on the high water, moving as close inshore as they can, rising and rolling steadily so they are both visible and vulnerable to a fly fisherman who follows them and keeps his fly over them. But when the tide begins to ebb the salmon retreat as quickly as they came on the flood, and soon they disappear as if they never had been there at all.

The steelhead's behavior is exactly the opposite; if there are any steelhead around at high tide you will never see them and it is almost useless to fish for them. They seem more patient than the salmon, less willing to press so far forward on the rising tide, more willing to wait for their destination stream to rise to a comfortable level. But they are also more stubborn than the salmon, and when the tide retreats they steadfastly refuse to go along with it; instead they hold their position, even if it means being temporarily trapped in a tidal pool with no escape until the tide returns. Once they find themselves in this situation, often in water so shallow it scarcely covers them, they begin to rise and porpoise nervously. This is the time they are most visible and vulnerable to anglers, but it's also usually long after most fishermen have quit fishing and gone home—for who would be foolish enough to stay and fish a minus tide? Unlikely as it seems, that is the very best of all times to fish for steelhead in the estuaries.

The shallow, clear water of a low or minus tide also often makes it possible for an angler to see everything—the fish, the fly, the follow, and the take—which elevates the experience to a whole new level of excitement. At this stage of their migration, when they have yet to make the transition from salt water into fresh, the steelhead also are usually in perfect condition, as fat and strong as they will ever be, and they are incredibly hot fish— twice the fish of any steelhead I have ever hooked in a river. The simile of hooking a lightning bolt was never more aptly applied than to hooking a steelhead in an estuary.

Perhaps part of this is because they are nearly all wild fish, fish destined for out-of-the-way little streams too small or unimportant for the state to worry about stocking with hatchery steelhead, streams whose steelhead runs are sustained only by natural spawning. This being so, I always try to treat estuary fish gently and release them as carefully as I can, hoping they will be able to go on safely to their spawning—for I know that killing even a single one could jeopardize the future run in a small stream where the spawning population might number less than twenty fish.

The technique I have found most successful for estuary steelhead is very similar to that employed by wet-fly trout fishermen in freshwater lakes. Using an intermediate (very slow sinking) line, a short leader with a breaking strength of eight pounds (six pounds in very clear water), and a bright fly, the technique is to cast randomly or to a specific rising fish, let the fly sink a little, then start a very fast retrieve. Sometimes the quick retrieve makes it difficult to hook a fish, but the steelhead seem much more responsive to a fast-moving fly than a slow one. On several occasions, when the water was calm and conditions seemed right, I also have succeeded in raising estuary fish to dry flies skated on the surface.

Over the years, during those infrequent winter dry spells, I have found several Puget Sound estuaries that produce consistent steelhead fishing, and I am certain there must be many more. But by far the best of any I have found is the secluded bay guarded by the Widow and her legions of chickens, cats, ponies, ducks, and dogs.

The finest day I ever had there also was one of the coldest. An overnight fog had deposited ice crystals on everything it touched, leaving all the meadows white, every young fir tree etched in silver, and the roads covered with black ice that made driving slippery and dangerous. The fog was just beginning to lift when I reached the Widow's place, and as it slowly dissolved it revealed a pale blue sky that promised a clear, cold day.

The usual thin strand of wood smoke was rising from the Widow's chimney when I pulled up to the gate, and the usual chorus of barking dogs brought her out for the usual front-porch confrontation. I got out of the truck, shivering in the cold morning air, and was surrounded quickly by the usual horde of sniffing dogs, waddling ducks, scratching chickens, and sneaking cats. Fortunately it was cold enough that even the Widow didn't seem to have much enthusiasm for conversation, and she soon bade me good day and retreated to the smelly warmth inside her house. Social obligations thus discharged, I gratefully escaped to the truck without even having been leaped upon, bitten, scratched, or pecked, and drove quickly down through the pasture to the launching area on the point.

Bundled up in long underwear, heavy shirt, thick sweater, and hooded jacket, I tossed my gear into the boat and shoved off. Once again I had chosen a day with a morning high tide followed by a long run-out due to end in a minus tide in late afternoon, and once again my plan was to search for cutthroat in the morning and steelhead in the afternoon. I checked out all the usual cutthroat haunts, but found nothing doing; if any cutthroat were about, they seemed unwilling to stick their noses up into the frigid air. The tide already was ebbing at a good clip, so after satisfying myself that the cutthroat were in hiding, I slipped anchor and again let the tidal flow carry me out of the bay and down to a spot just beyond the tip of the outer sand spit. I dropped anchor there in shallow water, out of the mainstream of the tidal current, and stood up to have a look around.

Nearby I saw a patch of long dark trailing weed on the bottom, each individual strand writhing gently in the tidal flow. I remember wishing idly they were fish instead of weeds—and then, on closer inspection through Polaroid glasses, I was startled to see that they were fish! What I had mistaken for strands of trailing weed was actually a school of about a dozen steelhead lying only twenty-five feet from my boat. As I looked around further I saw several other schools roaming restlessly off the little point where I had anchored.

For the next several hours I chased after them, cast over them, and peered intently through my Polaroids for the next sight of them whenever they moved on. I hooked four, losing the first on a spectacular jump and landing the next three, all chrome-bright, beautiful fish between six and eight pounds, strong and active and wild. By then it was late afternoon and time to start rowing back against the tide.

Again it was a tiring trip and I arrived off the Widow's point thinking only of the prospect of a restful trip home after a most satisfying day. But what happened next was a curious repeat of what had happened once before: A big fish rose not far away, and when I looked around I saw other rises and it was obvious the shallow tidal pool off the point again was filled with steelhead, more than I had ever seen there previously.

Thoughts of a restful trip home were quickly forgotten, and the next hour was a blur of furious activity. I quickly hooked two steelhead, each ten pounds or a little more, and landed both after a series of long blistering high-speed runs to the far corners of the pool where the oyster shells were just beginning to show above the tide. One of the fish also treated me to a series of high, spectacular, somersaulting leaps.

Both fish were absolutely wild—but neither as wild as the one that followed. It hit so hard the line cut into my finger and quickly drew blood, and instantly the fish was away on the longest, strongest, most powerful run I have ever experienced from any steelhead. It literally lunged through the water, breaking the surface time after time in a frantic dash far across the bay, and I watched with dismay as the backing whipped off the reel until the glimmer of metal spool appeared through the last few remaining turns. At that point I lifted the anchor to try to follow the fish, but by then it was far back in the half-submerged oyster beds, charging back and forth until there was a sudden snap, the line went slack, and I knew the fish was gone. For the next twenty minutes I followed a path of tangled line and backing through the oysters, freeing them up from all the places they had caught on the sharp, irregular edges of the oyster shells. If you can imagine a fish running into a field of freshly cooled volcanic lava, you will have some idea of the problem.

After that the last fish was something of an anticlimax, a nine-pounder that came to my fly just before darkness, jumped twice, but then mostly just sulked in the deepest part of the pool until I was finally able to winch it up to the boat and let it go. My final score for the day was eight steelhead hooked, six landed, and another half-dozen missed strikes—up to then, the best day of steelhead fishing I'd ever had.

So now, when winter comes, I no longer think much about going out in search of fishing room on the crowded rivers. I watch the weather forecasts instead, waiting and hoping for another of those rare midwinter dry spells—and with it perhaps another chance to find wild bright steelhead in the estuaries, waiting restlessly for the creeks to rise.

# 11 | STEELHEAD FLIES

T HE TRADITIONAL notion of a standard steelhead fly used to be that it should be made of gaudy and bright materials dressed heavily on a stout hook. Most of the flies used by early Northwest steelhead fishermen followed this formula, with thick bodies of chenille or wool in brilliant colors, usually ribbed with heavy bright tinsel and topped by bucktail or polar-bear wings, sometimes with waxy bright jungle-cock feathers added to the sides as a finishing touch. The theory behind these flies, if there was any conscious theory, was that they had to be dressed heavily with absorbent materials so they would soak up water quickly and sink down to the level of the fish; they also had to be bright in order to attract the steelhead's attention, especially in cloudy water.

At first there were not very many patterns, possibly because there were not very many fly fishermen, but it did not take very long for either of those things to change. In the late 1940s, when Enos Bradner was writing his book *Northwest Angling*, he remarked that "15 years ago there were very few patterns to choose

from; now there are dozens." Among those he listed as effective were the Orange Shrimp, Purple Peril, Brad's Brat (his own pattern), Killer, Skykomish Sunrise, Kalama Special, Lord Iris, Golden Demon, Lady Godiva, and Wind River Optic. Most of these were even more colorful than their names suggest.

Bright flies were still very much in vogue by the time I took up steelhead fly fishing, twenty years after the first edition of *Northwest Angling* was published. It was true that by then jungle-cock feathers had nearly disappeared from the market, polar-bear hair was becoming scarce, and flies made with either or both materials were not as common as they once had been. But as these natural materials became more difficult to obtain, new synthetic materials began to appear in their place, and innovative fly tyers soon found ways to incorporate them into their dressings. Most of the traditional patterns were still popular, even if substitute materials sometimes had to be used to tie them, and I stocked my fly boxes with patterns like the Skykomish Sunrise, Fall Favorite, Golden Demon, Skunk, and Omnibus. The Skykomish Sunrise was my favorite, partly because I loved its name but also because it was a beautiful and highly effective pattern, and I used it often in my early days of steelhead fishing.

No matter what patterns I used, all of them came from my own tying vise. I was still a very young, wet-behind-the-ears fly fisherman when I learned to tie flies, and books were my sole source of instruction because I did not then know anyone who might be able to teach me. Not surprisingly, my first efforts left much to be desired, and it was not uncommon for one of my patterns to shed a wing or a tail or some other crucial portion of its anatomy after only a few casts—which was rather discouraging considering it took about a half-hour for me to dress a single fly in those days. But I kept after it, and kept learning, and inevitably the products of my vise kept getting better and lasting longer and the trout began to accept them on a fairly regular basis, which pleased me no end.

But it was a long time before I learned enough about fly tying to realize that the books I had learned from had not necessarily been the best or the most recently published on the subject, and some of the methods I had acquired were obsolete long before I learned them. As a consequence, I had to face the reality that my tying techniques were neither very good nor very efficient—for example, I had never learned to tie with a bobbin. Unfortunately, by that time I had learned them all so well they had become second nature, habits so deeply ingrained that I found it very difficult to try to change them. In the end I decided not to change them and went on using my bumbling old methods, discovering as I did so that I felt no particular loss of enjoyment from fly tying even though my techniques might be awkward or out of date. Besides, even if my flies were not always of exhibition quality, the trout seemed to like them well enough.

The transition from trout flies to steelhead patterns also seemed to go easily enough at first. Certainly the steelhead hooks were a little larger than I was accustomed to working with, and some of the materials were a little different, but most of the techniques were the same, and it did not take very long to tie enough flies to fill my boxes with all the traditional patterns I felt I had to have—the Skykomish Sunrises, Fall Favorites, and so forth. But after I had tied all those well-established and well-defined patterns, I was at a loss to know quite what to do next—and that led me to contemplate the major difference between tying trout flies and steelhead patterns.

In trout fishing the fly tyer's objective almost always is to fashion a pattern that closely resembles an insect or some other natural organism in appearance, behavior, or both. The natural offers the tyer a model, and if he is successful in imitating that model he is likely to seduce a lot of trout. But steelhead returning to the rivers rarely feed consistently, if at all, so in most cases there is no natural model for a steelhead fly tyer to try to imitate. Without the logic and discipline of imitation to guide him, things are pretty much left up to the tyer's imagination, and experiments with steelhead flies usually involve concocting random patterns in various colors, shapes, and textures, then trying them out to see which, if any, provoke a favorable response from the fish.

Certainly there's nothing wrong in that; in fact, it can be great fun. And some fly tyers probably would argue that it gives them more freedom than the discipline imposed by the necessity for "matching the hatch" in trout fishing. But such abstract, free-form experimentation doesn't appeal to me quite as much as tying trout flies because both inclination and past experience serve to point me in the direction of imitation and its greater basis in logic and practicality. Or, to put it another way, I suppose my attitude toward fly tying is more utilitarian than abstract or artistic.

Not that that attitude has kept me from experimenting with steelhead patterns; far from it. Once I figured out there were no imitative models to emulate in tying steelhead flies, I started experimenting with wet-fly patterns in various combinations of materials and colors and textures. Some of these flies were pretty weird and most of them were unsuccessful, at least in terms of attracting fish, and that general lack of success probably has played a subconscious role in making me feel more comfortable tying imitative flies for trout than abstract patterns for steelhead.

Fortunately for all of us, other steelhead fly tyers have been more successful, and the lack of imitative models has not inhibited them from using their imaginations in highly creative ways. The late Syd Glasso developed a series of spey-hackle steelhead patterns that were beautiful and graceful masterpieces of the fly tyer's art—as well as highly effective takers of steelhead. George Keough, another late friend, invented what he called "the Floss Fly," a curious creation in which two flies were tied at once by winding strands of brightly colored floss around parallel hooks set in separate vises. The floss was cemented in place along each hook shank with epoxy glue and the strands were then cut in the middle so that the Siamese twin flies were separated. The result was a pair of patterns with floss hanging down like fringe from the hook shanks—floss was the only material used—and although they looked ugly in the hand, they fluttered like bright pennants in the river and caught steelhead with uncommon frequency.

In each case these flies relied mostly upon the movement of

the materials—the spey hackle in Glasso's flies, the strands of floss in Keough's—for their attractive qualities. Quite a different approach was taken by Walt Johnson, whose elegant Red Shrimp, Orange Shrimp, and Prawn patterns were based on the theory that steelhead in rivers might respond to flies that resembled organisms they had eaten at sea. This brought imitation back to steelhead patterns, but ignored conventional stream insects to concentrate instead on naturals encountered by steelhead during their ocean feeding experience—and the imitations tended to be more abstract than exact.

I admire these and other innovative approaches to wet-fly pattern development, but my own steelhead fly-tying experiments have been concentrated mostly on floating patterns in recent years, a reflection of my preference for fishing dry flies.

Since I fish riffle-hitched flies most often, most of my experiments have been devoted to patterns that work best with that method. And here again my past trout-fishing experience has exerted a powerful influence on the direction I have taken, evident in the fact that most of my steelhead dry flies closely resemble standard trout patterns in basic design. Among others, I have experimented with Muddler-type patterns, flat-winged flies, and the sort of "giant Adams" upright hairwinged style that brought me my first steelhead on a dry fly. The latter has proven consistently best for my purposes.

Usually I tie these flies on #6 long-shanked low-water Atlantic salmon hooks. The pattern, as it has evolved over time, calls for long fibers of dark deer body hair to be bound parallel to the hook shank so that their tips extend aft of the bend, providing a tail for the fly, while their hollow air-filled midsections serve to add a core of flotation to the body, which will be added later. The wing is a much larger clump of dark deer body hair, tied in upright fashion about three-sixteenths of an inch behind the eye of the hook. The body is added next, and usually I choose peacock herl, wool, fur dubbing, or sparkle yarn in a variety of colors, although basic black remains my favorite. The body material is wound over the deer-hair core covering the hook shank and forward as far as the wing, with a single turn in front of the wing. Then two stiff hackle feathers are tied in and wrapped on either side of the wing to give it stability. The color of the hackles may be varied to suit the color of the body—brown or grizzly-and-brown mixed for lighter colors, natural black to match the black body that I usually tie.

This pattern is designed so that the riffle hitch can be tied behind the wing, rather than in front as is ordinarily the case, and the fly-to-leader connection is therefore only a little bit forward of the center of the hook. The result is that the fly always rides at a sharp angle to the current, which helps keep it afloat and adds to the disturbance or wake it leaves as it skates across the surface. The high deer-hair wing also makes the fly readily visible, even in smaller sizes (a #10 hook is the smallest size I use for this pattern). On those occasions when I raise a fish to a fly of one color and miss the strike, as often happens, changing to a different size or different color often results in another rise—and when the rise is expected, and the fish actually takes, the strike is rarely missed.

At various times I have thought up names for this series of flies, but none seems to have stuck well enough to be remembered from season to season. So it remains a nameless pattern.

I have enjoyed a great deal of success raising steelhead with this upright-wing pattern, but there is another floating fly I consider even more effective at bringing fish to the surface—although, unfortunately, it is not nearly as good at hooking them. This is the Bomber, a pattern originally developed for Atlantic salmon. Usually it is tied with a body of spun clipped deer hair, a palmered brown or red hackle, and a shellback wing of white calf tail or bucktail extending into a short tail at the aft end of the fly and ending in a sort of topknot at the front end, just over the eye.

The great virtue of this fly is that it will float through almost anything, and the little topknot in front helps create a surface disturbance even if the fly is fished without a riffle hitch. It has a low silhouette and rides much lower in the water than my upright-wing pattern, which makes it more difficult for a fisherman to see—but steelhead apparently have no trouble seeing it, and some of the most spectacular steelhead rises I have ever witnessed have been to a Bomber. But the bulk of its clipped deer-hair body—the very thing that makes it float so well—also restricts its hooking qualities because it seems no matter how carefully the body is trimmed there is still never quite enough of a gap between the hook point and the body of the fly to give the hook much purchase. For that reason I use the Bomber most often as a searching fly, then switch to one of my own patterns if the Bomber succeeds in bringing a fish to the surface.

I suppose my lack of success in developing wet patterns is another reason most of my steelhead experiments have been with floating flies. Certainly the failure to score a hit with a wet pattern has scarcely been an inducement to continue trying. Instead, I have left that end of things to my son, Randy, who managed to score a hit on one of his very first tries.

Randy began learning to tie flies at the age of six, looking over my shoulder to watch what I was doing and asking questions incessantly. When his interest became apparent I gave him an old vise and some hand-me-down materials, which he soon augmented with purchases of his own and frequent raids on the contents of my fly-tying box. With the aid of some able third-party instruction, he soon learned to tie flies using the modern methods I had never been taught, and progressed rapidly from the stage of the hopeless snarl to the point where he was able to dress very respectable patterns. Even so, I was still surprised one Christmas morning when I opened a package and found inside a large selection of steelhead patterns he had tied for me. Mostly they were his original creations, based on nothing more than imagination, and some were pretty fanciful. But all were nicely tied and some looked quite interesting, so I put a few of them in one of the fly boxes I carry in my steelhead vest.

A couple of weeks after Christmas I went fishing and decided to try one of Randy's patterns—an extraordinarily bright fly with a fluorescent hot-orange chenille body and matching marabou tail and wing. A steelhead of about six and a half pounds thought enough of the fly to take it, and when I landed the fish I decided to keep it with the fly still stuck in its jaw so I could take it home and show it to Randy. But as I was leaving the stream, carrying the fish in one hand, I was stopped by a game warden who wanted to check my license. The warden noticed the fly in the steelhead's mouth and asked the name of the pattern. I told him it didn't have one, that it was just a fly my son had cooked up from materials on hand.

"Well, then" the warden said, "I think you should name it after your son."

I thought that was a very good idea. But naming a fly isn't something you should do on the spur of the moment; it's a matter that requires some careful thought. After all, a good fly deserves a good name, something colorful and descriptive, perhaps something alliterative, and of course the name also should give proper recognition to the author of the pattern. After I got home I discussed all this with Randy but we didn't come to any immediate conclusion, so I decided I would simply call the new fly Randy's Pattern until one of us could think of a better name. Besides, a single fish was scarcely enough to assure the success of a new pattern, and the fly would take a lot more proving before it could truly be considered worthy of a name of its own.

Two weeks later I went fishing again and hooked six steelhead, one of the best days of winter fishing I'd ever had. All six fish took Randy's Pattern, and when I gave one of his flies to a friend fishing nearby he quickly broke it off in a steelhead. This seemed more than just coincidence, and I began to think that Randy might really have hit on something.

Next weekend I went out again—and hooked eight steelhead on Randy's Pattern. By this time there was no doubt in my mind that the fly had some mysterious elusive quality that steelhead found irresistible and I knew it was a fly I would always want to have in my box. Furthermore, if any steelhead fly pattern ever earned the honor of having its own name, it seemed to me that this one surely had.

So Randy and I had another discussion about an appropriate

name. I held out for something traditional and alliterative, suggesting "Randy's Reliable" or "Randy's Renegade." The fly's author accepted the idea of alliteration but otherwise balked at my proposals on the grounds that they were far too conservative and conventional. Instead, he went to the dictionary and spent a good deal of time looking through all the words beginning with the letter R, searching for one he thought would be ideally suited for the purpose. At length he announced that his fly would be known as "Randy's Retiary," which in turn sent me to the dictionary to find out what in the world retiary meant. I learned that it means "to be equipped with a net," and I suppose to Randy the net simile seemed an apt measure of the effectiveness of his new fly. At any rate, "Randy's Retiary" it was and is.

Not very long after this I was asked to give a talk and show a film on fishing to the men's group at a local church. I invited Randy to come along, suggesting he could demonstrate his fly-tying skills, which he willingly agreed to do. During my brief talk I mentioned his new fly and how I had so far used it to hook fifteen steelhead in three outings. Then Randy set up his vise and the audience gathered around to watch him and ignored me for the rest of the evening. At the end of the program the chairman of the men's group offered Randy a cash honorarium, which he gratefully accepted; I was offered their sincere thanks.

Of course the whole experience tickled me greatly, and it taught Randy that fly tying could be remunerative as well as enjoyable. Since then he has picked up more than a little spending money filling orders for custom-tied flies, and I remain one of his best customers. His Retiary has gone on to prove its worth not only for steelhead but also for chinook and coho salmon, sea-run cutthroat, Dolly Varden, and landlocked Atlantic salmon, and I carry more of them in my fly boxes than any other pattern.

(Another of Randy's experiments unfortunately did not turn out as well. This was a pattern he christened the "Aspersion" in hopes that one day another fisherman would ask him what fly he was using and he could answer, "I've been casting Aspersions." But it hasn't happened yet.)

Along with the Retiary I also still carry some traditional old favorites in my collection of wet-fly patterns. An underwater snag took my last Skykomish Sunrise some time ago and I haven't yet bothered to replace it, but my fly boxes still contain a full supply of Skunks and Fall Favorites, plus half a dozen copies each of the Omnibus and the Oso Special.

The Skunk is a ubiquitous steelhead fly throughout the Northwest, perhaps throughout the entire natural range of the steelhead; certainly it is the most popular dark steelhead pattern in existence, although nobody seems to remember who created it, or exactly when or where. The Fall Favorite is an old British Columbia pattern and I love it for its pleasing colors and simple, elegant lines—and also because it is one of the most effective flies I know, fished just beneath the surface on an oft-mended floating line.

The Omnibus is an old pattern of Len Hunton's, developed for steelhead and cutthroat in the sluggish rivers and estuaries of Willapa Bay. It is a fly that combines both bright and dark colors with good movement in the water, and it remains the best pattern I know for moving a difficult fish that has refused all other offerings. The Oso Special is a relative newcomer, introduced to me by Rod Belcher, a local sports broadcaster and occasional fishing companion. Named after the little community where Deer Creek flows into the North Fork of the Stillaguamish, it is a big, ugly, simple fly that I don't much like either to tie or to fish—but it works, especially when the water in the North Fork is turbid, as it has been so often in recent years.

Whenever I fish a wet fly, as I now do less and less often, it is usually one of these four patterns or Randy's Retiary. Whenever I fish a floating fly, as I now do most of the time, the choice usually is a Bomber or one of my nameless upright hairwing patterns. So nearly all of my steelhead fishing is done with only these seven patterns—but in my fishing vest I still carry four boxes crammed full of several dozen patterns, both wet and dry. These are flies I have been given or bought or tied at one time or another but that I use rarely, if ever. There is nothing wrong with any of them except that I lack confidence in them because I have never given them a fair chance to prove themselves. I could probably get along easily without them, but I would never think of leaving them behind; the time may yet come when my pet patterns will fail me and one of the many flies tucked away in my boxes will emerge from obscurity to spell the difference between victory and defeat.

In this feeling I suspect I am no different from most fishermen. I tend to stay with the flies I know and trust from years of experience, ignoring the others in my box—even though they constitute the majority—but I would never want to face the prospect of going fishing without them. They are my security blanket, my reinforcements if the frontline flies should ever fail, and I feel better having them with me.

Recent years have brought many exciting new developments in steelhead fly-dressing theory and practice. The rapid proliferation of fly-fishing clubs, magazines, and books has for the first time given tyers an opportunity to share their findings and experiences, even though they may be separated by great distances, and progress has been much faster than it was in the days when most fly dressers worked in isolation. The development of new synthetics also has allowed tyers to devise many new patterns based on materials that did not even exist a few years ago.

Along with this renaissance in steelhead fly-pattern development has come a trend to experiment with new or revised techniques of presentation. The increasing use of double-handed fly rods, made possible by the revolution in fly-rod technology, is one example, and I have already mentioned the interesting results some anglers have obtained fishing upstream for steelhead with tiny weighted nymphs, or by rolling large stonefly-nymph imitations along the bottom.

Other fishermen have fashioned new "waking" flies designed specifically to cause the maximum possible commotion on the surface, while yet others have experimented successfully with very large floating flies intended to imitate swimming mice or voles. At least one British Columbia angler has gone sharply in the opposite direction, reporting the successful capture of a steelhead on a size 20 dry fly.

All of these are exciting developments, and while I can hardly say that I have been close to the forefront of any of them, I find all of them promising and interesting. I may even try to take advantage of some of them, although I have been fishing for steelhead long enough now that I find myself growing somewhat set in my ways and increasingly content to stay with them—and in that sense, I suppose, I am still partly a captive of the tradition under which I learned to fish.

Nevertheless, I would be first to endorse all the changes that have taken place since the days when steelhead patterns were few and any pattern was considered good if it was bright and sank easily. The problem today is not with fly patterns, but with the fact that there are not nearly as many steelhead as there were just twenty or thirty years ago—and the few steelhead remaining are fished over so heavily that they quickly grow wary and wise. So the fly patterns of the future may have to be even better than those of today in order to be effective in raising these well-educated fish.

Still, it is an exciting time for a steelhead fly fisher to be alive, particularly if he or she is young, because today's new fly patterns and the new methods for fishing them hold nothing but bright promise for the future. I would never want to trade my memories of the past—but it's hard not to feel a touch of envy of those who are just getting started.

# 12 | THE COMPLEAT STEELHEADER

THE SEASONS slip past quickly now, and it is astonishing to realize that nearly a quarter of a century has passed since I first took up a fly rod and went out searching for steelhead. A great many miles of river have passed underfoot since those early days, and virtually each one of them has meant new lessons learned and new understanding gained.

I think, over time, that almost every fisherman develops something akin to a monogamous relationship with a favorite river, a river he loves and knows more intimately and desires to fish above all others. And so I have done, choosing the North Fork of the Stillaguamish for my home river and pledging to stick with it come what may. But there is nothing that requires an angler to forsake all rivers but one, and like most fishermen I still have the instinctive urge to explore and sample new waters from time to time. So in recent years I have continued to add to my collection of rivers, both near and far from home.

One of these, in a sense, was not wholly unfamiliar. For many years I have fished the upper reaches of the Sauk River in late summer, always above its confluence with the glacial Whitechuck. The Whitechuck's milky effluent keeps the lower Sauk flowing perpetually opaque and gray through July and August, and although I had driven often along the river's lower reaches to scout the water, I had never found it even remotely fishable during months when the summer steelhead were in. Sometimes I had seen it clear in winter, when the weather was cold enough to stem the flow from the glacier that feeds the Whitechuck, but usually it was then so crowded with anglers there was little room left for a fly fisherman. But a few years ago the state declared a catch-and-release season on the lower Sauk during March and April, when the big native winter steelhead return to the river. The new regulations discouraged both bait fishermen and meat fishermen, which left more room for everyone else, and fly fishermen soon began to take advantage of the situation.

That was how it happened one night in early March that I received a phone call from Alec Jackson, who reported the lower Sauk was in prime shape and that he and Bob Aid had each taken a fish the day before. I needed no further encouragement, and next morning I set out for the lower river. There had been a hard overnight frost, but it soon dissolved in a wonderfully clear, springlike morning. Columns of thick white wood smoke rose from the chimney of nearly every house and cabin along the road to the river, and every hilltop was crowned with bright fresh snow. Whitehorse Mountain was sparkling and spectacular in the morning sunshine, the usual harsh outlines of its rugged crags softened by a smooth, heavy snowfall that extended nearly all the way down to the valley floor. It was one of those rare mornings when the air has an electric tingle that fills you with high energy and gladness to be a part of it.

I drove to the spot Alec had mentioned, where he and Bob had hooked their fish, but found it already occupied by other fishermen, so I turned back upstream a short distance and pulled off at a place where the river swung well away from the road and it was a fair hike down to the water. Walking blindly through the woods to an unfamiliar stretch of river always poses a risk that you may strike it at a point where there is no good water for fishing, but it also greatly reduces the chance that you will find others already fishing there, so the risk was one I was willing to take.

I put on my waders and put up my rod, scrambled down the steep bank next to the road, and entered the woods. It was like stepping into another world, a dark and silent world with the sky closed off by the thick overhead foliage of gnarled old cedars and stately firs. The ground underfoot was covered with moss, a foot thick or more it seemed, and walking on it was like walking on the softest carpet; there was no trail, but the going was easy through patches of fern and salal and around old fallen moss-covered logs. Long beards of moss also trailed from the lower limbs of the cedars and touched me lightly as I passed. I quickly lost sight of the highway and there was no sound either from it or from the river, but I pressed on ahead, relying on an intuitive sense of direction.

After a ten- or fifteen-minute walk I could hear the diffused sound of the river up ahead and soon stepped out of the woods at the edge of a lovely long pool fed by braided chutes of fast water. As I had expected, there were no other fishermen present and the only footprints in the sand along the riverbank had been left by deer. I picked up some fallen limbs and fashioned them in the shape of an arrow to mark the spot where I had left the woods so I could find my way back when I was through fishing, then went down to take a closer look at the river. It held only the slightest touch of color, like a deep green emerald flawed with streaks of silver, transparent and mysterious with the sun striking sparks from every break in the braided current. On the opposite shore the buds were just rising in the woods, giving the alders and willows a fresh blush of mint color that was in pleasing contrast to the darker green of fir and cedar in the deeper woods beyond and the bright blue sky overhead. It was a wonderful place and I felt wonderful being there.

The river sipped and sighed as it slipped over boulders and bright gravel and the water was icy cold as I stepped into it. I had thought the water would be cold, probably too cold for a fish to rise willingly to a dry fly, so I had chosen a sinking-tip line and a large wet fly, and as I waded out the first few steps confirmed that at least I had been right about the water temperature. I began fishing at the head of the pool, though the river was so wide I could cover scarcely half of it even with the longest double-hauled cast. But there was more than enough of interest to keep me fully occupied in the area I could reach, and I had to mend the sink-tip line busily to work the fly around the dark shapes of boulders under water.

I had fished down perhaps a hundred yards when I saw a steel-head roll on the far side of the river. It was a large fish and the sun had caught its thick side briefly as it breached the surface. It was lying in a perfect spot, in deep water with a little knuckle of current showing on the surface. But it was a long way away, and I waded out farther in hopes of getting within casting range. The bottom shelved steeply and the current grew stronger with every outward step I took until soon the water was close to my wader tops; its coldness took my breath away and its strength plucked and pulled at my legs until I knew I could go no farther. Without much hope for the results, I tried a cast from where I was, work-ing hard to double-haul and shoot line until finally I let go and watched as the fly fell frustratingly short of its target.

Several more times I tried, but the fish was simply beyond reach. Just as I was about to admit defeat and make the difficult pivot to start wading back, the steelhead rolled again, its sides once more flashing briefly in the sunlight. It was in exactly the same place as before, and although the second sight of it encouraged me to try casting several times more, the results were still the same.

I waded out and walked around on the shore for a while to restore circulation and warmth to my frozen limbs, then returned to the long pool and fished through the rest of it, paused to change flies, and then went through again, still without moving a fish. By then the short late-winter day was nearly spent, the western sky was turning salmon red, and it was time to go. I found the arrow I had made from broken limbs and hiked back through the woods to my car, empty-handed but full of bright memories and a fresh love for the lower Sauk. And since then I have returned to it as often as I could.

Another river of recent acquaintance, one much farther from home, is the mighty Taku of British Columbia and Alaska. The Taku gathers the runoff of countless tributaries from a huge area of northern British Columbia and carries it in a great sprawling watery highway down through an enormous canyon past the feet of a half-dozen glaciers until it finally reaches the inside passage near Juneau; in turn the river draws to itself magnificent runs of spring steelhead and summer salmon.

It was the prospect of spring steelhead that brought me to the Taku along with Errol Champion, Bill Corbus, Dick Deems, and C. B. Bettisworth, all residents of the Juneau area. We crammed our gear into a pair of jet boats skippered by Bill and C.B. and set out from Juneau on a raw day in early May, running forty miles to the spot where the Taku hisses and boils over the huge shifting sandbars it has built for itself at its exit to the sea. En route we enjoyed a great panorama of mountains rising steeply from the waves, a seemingly endless succession of rocky ridges like giant ocean swells frozen into stone. Their lower slopes were clad in dusky spruce, their summits all barren and rocky and windswept, and along their creviced sides long ribbons of bright snow streaked down to the water. In the troughs between the mountains were deep valleys filled by hunchbacked glaciers with cold blue veins and an icy breath that numbed our faces.

As we skimmed over the water we could see seals and sea lions everywhere, their wedged-shaped heads bobbing to the surface like animated flotsam. Eagles circled overhead, almost as numerous as starlings back home, and at a distance we saw a great humpback whale heave itself out of the water and fall back in an enormous white wave, the sound of its mighty splash echoing long off the rocky hillsides.

Then we were into the river itself, running thick and brown with soil leached from the distant hills of the interior but still flowing swift and cold and strong. At the end of a long run we reached our first night's destination, a Forest Service cabin on the lower river. Next morning we started early and soon passed the ugly defoliated line that marks the border between Alaska and British Columbia, then continued upstream through a narrowing valley that eventually grew into a canyon with mountains pressing in closely on either side, and through binoculars we could see mountain goats like clusters of snowberry on the distant alpine slopes. As we headed farther into the interior the canyon opened up into a valley once again, although not as wide as before, and we ran swiftly past great unbroken forests of spruce, cottonwood, and birch until at midafternoon we reached our destination at the mouth of a major tributary, perhaps a hundred miles from where we had started.

There we were greeted by a deeply disappointing sight: A major portion of the Taku's mud-brown stain was coming from the tributary we had planned to fish, a river normally clear at this season. An unusual early spell of warm weather had prematurely melted the snowfields in its headwater mountains, and now runoff was rapidly filling the river.

We had allowed ourselves three days to fish; instead we spent them hiking the trails around camp, visiting a curious old Tlingit Indian graveyard on a nearby hilltop, or sitting around a smoldering campfire trading stories while we watched and waited for the river to drop. But it never dropped; instead it rose even higher until it was nearly bank-full and roaring by the time we had to leave, and we started downstream in company with chunks of ice and last winter's timber deadfalls, tossing and turning in the standing waves of the torrent.

The strength of the runoff added to our speed so that it seemed as if the jet boats fairly flew on the downstream journey, although we stopped several times to cast hopefully into little patches of clear water near the mouths of several smaller tributaries. We caught nothing but Dolly Varden, and as it happened the butcher in Juneau who had made up our order for the trip had shorted us one day's supply of meat, so we ended up eating Dolly Varden for dinner on the final night of the trip. The Dolly is scarcely a gourmand's fish, but at least we were not hungry.

So the Taku and its tributaries kept their secrets from me, although I will always remember that wild and magnificent country—and perhaps, someday, I will have a chance to go back and will find the rivers flowing clear.

A much smaller river, and one much closer to home, is the little Coquihalla, which flows out of the mountains of southern British Columbia to merge with the Fraser River near the town of Hope. The Coquihalla is a river that has taken much more than its share of abuse over the years, having suffered the effects of mining, logging, a railroad, an oil pipeline, and, most recently, the construction of a superhighway that required rerouting the river channel more than twenty times. Not surprisingly, all these activities took a fearful toll on the Coquihalla's native steelhead run, long ago reducing it to the point of extinction. But restoration efforts and careful nurturing by provincial biologists have succeeded in reestablishing a run that, if not founded entirely on the river's native stock, still has made the Coquihalla a river once again worth fishing.

Before most of the sad things happened to it, the Coquihalla was the river of Tommy Brayshaw, the "ardent angler-artist" whose beautiful and graceful trout and salmon illustrations graced the pages of Roderick Haig-Brown's books and still decorate the walls of many angling dens, and whose amazingly life-like fish carvings are a source of wonder to all who behold them.

The Coquihalla was the river on which Brayshaw developed a series of small but elegant steelhead flies—Brayshaw's Black-and-White, the Coquihalla Orange, and Coquihalla Silver—which he fashioned carefully in his fingers, without the aid of a vise.

Despite all that has happened to it since, it is hard to fish the Coquihalla without thinking of Tommy. Like him, the river is small and quick and lively, always chuckling, its bright riffles sparkling as his eyes sparked with humor and wisdom. Seldom has a river been so perfectly matched to the personality of the man who fished it, and although the Coquihalla never again will resemble the pristine river that Tommy Brayshaw knew, it is easy and tempting to believe that perhaps some part of his spirit remains there, revived each year when wary, ghost-gray steelhead slip back into the river in late July or early August and wait to take a well-presented fly.

The Sauk, the Taku, the Coquihalla—these and other rivers all tempt me from time to time, tempt me enough to take me away from my home water on the North Fork of the Stillaguamish. But I always return to the North Fork because that is where I feel most comfortable and confident, most closely in tune with my surroundings, most free to think about fishing and all the things that are a part of it. And lately, with the sad decline of the North Fork fishery, there has been plenty of time for such thinking.

It is relaxing while fishing to let one's thoughts roam in random patterns, to let ideas, memories, and images come and go in infinite variety like dreams in the night. But no matter how far afield my thoughts may roam, they always return eventually to fishing—the fishing that I am doing, or have done, or still hope to do. And among the things I think about most often is what it all means, and what it takes, to be a steelhead fly fisherman.

I suppose one reason I think about this is because of the questions I am now asked more and more frequently by younger fishermen just starting out in pursuit of steelhead. They want to know what skills are needed to become a "compleat" steelhead fly fisherman and how to go about learning them, and it is a flattering thing to be asked because implicit in the question is the assumption that I must know the answer. Usually I reply with a list of fairly obvious things, but always afterwards I am bothered by a disturbing feeling I have left out something very important.

The truth is that there is much I do not know about steelhead fly fishing and probably never shall know. Many anglers know more, and will always know more, because they fish more often than I do, fish only for steelhead, and pursue them with a fierce singleness of purpose that excludes anything and everything else. I cannot compete for their knowledge or fishing time or intensity, for even as much as I love steelhead I also care deeply for the abundance of other kinds of fishing that my native Northwest has to offer. So in the spring, when the hatches are on, I fish most often not for steelhead but for trout, and I do so again in the fall after the first frosts, when the trout are fat and active and the crowds are gone. I fish for salmon wherever and whenever I can, and for sea-run cutthroat in the winter, and sometimes in summer I will take time to visit an alpine lake in search of brook trout. But summers mostly are reserved for steelhead, along with several weekends in the fall and any winter day when I can get away and the rivers are clear and uncrowded or the creeks low enough to hold the promise of steelhead in the estuaries. It is satisfying to be able to fish so many different kinds of water for so many different kinds of fish, and I love the variety, but one cost of such pragmatic angling habits is that I will never know as much about steelhead fly fishing as those who devote all their time and attention to it.

Some fishermen literally dedicate their lives to the pursuit of steelhead. They fish five, six, or sometimes even seven days a week, and so of course they see more and learn more than anyone who does not fish that often. I have met such men from time to time in fishing camps or along rivers, angling nomads who move from stream to stream or from lower river to upper river, depending on how the water is and where the fish are in. They are invariably bachelors, either because they always have been or because they gave up marriage in favor of steelhead—steelhead can do that to a man—and they work only when their food supply runs low and they need to earn a little money to buy more, or perhaps to buy a new rod or a new line, which may well come higher than food on their shopping lists.

To them a river is like a residential street—it is where they live, usually in the back of an old station wagon with a sleeping bag and a cooler full of beer and cheese, and perhaps a dog for company—and any time they must spend away from a river usually is time spent unwillingly. They have been called steelhead bums, which is an accurate but not very flattering term, and I suspect the unflattering nature of it may well be due to envy on the part of us who call them that. They have given up all the comforts and cultural attractions of city life, eschewed all the amenities of family and domestic existence, and dismissed all notion of material wealth to devote themselves to the single-minded pursuit of steelhead—and yet they always seem to have as much as they need, and perhaps more than the rest of us. Certainly they catch a lot more fish than I do and know much more about steelhead fly fishing than I will ever know.

Yet I do not think that even these extraordinary fishermen are in any sense "compleat" steelheaders. They are still learning, too, as fishermen always must learn, for there is no end to the things we must and should know. And even in the highly unlikely event that someday we should know everything, or find the answers to all our angling questions, we probably would still disagree over the meaning of the answers and be no better off than before.

But having said all that, I still feel compelled to try to tackle the question of what it takes to be a good steelhead fisherman, if only to present a more true account to those for whom I have tried to answer the question on other occasions. My answer is necessarily based on incomplete knowledge and reflects my own angling prejudices, and it is only one answer among many that might be given; but I will say in its defense that it reflects nearly a generation's worth of steelhead fly-fishing experience and a not inconsiderable amount of thought devoted to the subject.

To begin with, a successful steelhead fly fisherman must be endowed with the virtue of infinite patience. This, of course, has always been true for any kind of fishing; indeed, as far back as 1577 William Samuel wrote in *The Arte of Angling* that a successful angler must have "faith, believing that there is fish." But today's steelhead fishermen must have an extra store of such faith, a much greater willingness to "believe that there is fish"—for the number of steelhead seems to dwindle constantly, for many reasons, while the number of anglers fishing for them is ever on the increase.

Thus for a steelhead fisherman in today's context, patience means the ability and willingness to go for long periods—days or sometimes even weeks—without a strike or a rise or even a single sign of fish, yet without ever giving up hope that the very next cast may result in a slashing take that will erase the memory of all the weeks of waiting. It also means having the patience to put up with crowded streams and the occasional thoughtlessness of other anglers, with increasingly common no-trespassing signs and crowded access areas, and with long waiting lines on the best fishing drifts.

It means, too, being patient with other users of the river, the kayakers and boaters and tubers and swimmers and others who so often get in the way of anglers and disturb their sport even though fishermen pose no conceivable threat of interference in return. Admittedly it is very difficult to maintain patience in the face of such provocations, but if one is charitable enough he can perhaps be forgiving on the grounds that most of these people probably know not what they do.

But there is a limit even to the infinite patience that a good steelhead fisherman must have. For instance, there is no reason at all to be patient with those who deliberately abuse rivers and do so with full knowledge of the consequences of their acts, despite what they may say. I speak of those who set their own selfish short-term economic gain above the health of rivers—the logging companies, the polluters, the real-estate "developers," and all their ilk—and the sneaking poachers who would rob the rivers of their runs. For them we should have nothing but contempt, and for their schemes nothing but opposition.

The next requirement for a good steelhead angler is skill, an obvious thing, and it includes skill in casting, in line handling, in wading, and in streamcraft. Skill in casting means knowing not only how to cast, but where and when and how often; it means knowing the roll cast, the backhand cast, the slack-line cast, and other specialized casts for specialized situations. Skill in line handling means knowing not only how to mend line, but when, how often, and in which direction—and when it is better not to mend at all.

Skill in wading means knowing not only how to wade, but when and where, and how to extricate oneself from the precarious situations that are bound to arise. Skill in streamcraft means knowing how to decipher the subtle messages written in the current's changing scrawl, knowing which small sections of all the long river are likely to hold fish, and how to reach whatever fish may be holding there.

All these things can be learned from practice and experience, from careful observation and constant attention, from thought and deduction and perception and imagination. Books help; books offer clues and suggestions and a solid base upon which to build a greater knowledge. But books by themselves never can hold or offer all or even most of the answers a steelhead fisherman needs.

The best thing about steelhead fly-fishing skills is that they are as pleasant to acquire as they are to apply. All the learning, all the practice, all the doing, all the observation and attention and reading and thought, everything that must be done to acquire and polish good fishing skills—all these are also plain, unadulterated fun, things that would be worth doing for their own enjoyment even if we learned nothing from them. The fact that we do learn from them, and that we are later able to employ the knowledge effectively for ourselves, simply adds to the enjoyment.

The next requirement is knowledge, which is different from skill. A good steelhead fly fisher should have a good knowledge of the fish he seeks. He should know as much about the steelhead as he can learn, about its birth in the river, its early perilous life in the shallows, its long dangerous journey downstream to the sea; about its migrations and ocean feeding and the instinctive desire that eventually causes it to turn once more toward home; about its long return and all the natural hazards and manmade threats it must survive to reach its native river; and above all about its ascent of that river and its habits and preferences and where and when and at what stage of the water it is likely to travel or rest, and to what fly it is most likely to respond.

Like the mechanical skills of steelhead fly fishing, these things also are best learned by long practice and observation, although perhaps more of them are revealed by books or nature study. The best place to begin is to go out on a winter river and witness the spawning of wild steelhead, which discloses both the beginning and the end of the steelhead's magnificent cycle of life; if that is not possible, then it is almost equally instructive to go and watch how steelhead are spawned artificially in a hatchery. Since it is almost never possible to watch wild fry emerging from the gravel of a river, a hatchery also is a good place to watch as the fertile eggs miraculously become squirming alevins, then mature quickly into silvery, active fry. In the hatchery, too, you can visit young steelhead as often as you wish and watch them as they grow to smolting size; perhaps you can even arrange to be there to bid them Godspeed on the day of their release to the river. And in a year or two or three, if you are lucky, you may even catch one on its return.

Of course the environment of the hatchery is artificial and protects the young from most of the menaces their wild counterparts must endure, but it is as close as most people can get to witnessing the real thing. Unfortunately, catching returning adults spawned in the hatcheries also is more and more often as close as most people can get to the real thing. Many anglers resent this, contending that hatchery steelhead are as artificial as the environment in which they were reared, that they are the result of genetic manipulation rather than natural selection, robbed before birth of the best aspects of their native character, raised under false pretenses and unworthy of comparison in behavior or sporting quality with their native brethren in the wild. This argument is mostly subjective, but there is also more than a little factual evidence to support it, and some fishermen have carried it to the extreme of insisting there should be no hatchery fish at all. In a perfect world I would be quick to agree, but since the world is far from perfect and its number of wild steelhead grows smaller every year, I would rather have hatchery steelhead than none at all.

I will always hope, as all anglers should, for the survival, restoration and growth of wild steelhead runs wherever they still exist. But as a practical matter, I think many if not most of our future steelhead will have to come from hatcheries, and while we should never relax in our defense of wild runs, we should also spend more time and attention working to improve hatchery stocks and hatchery methods.

There is another important quality that I think a good steelhead fisherman must have, and that is a feeling of appreciation

and respect—appreciation for the fish, for the river, for all the life in and around and above the river, for the woods along its shores, for the mountains that give it birth, and for the great blessing of being in the middle of all these things. If one has such appreciation then respect will naturally follow, a healthy respect for all of these things and for the tradition of the sport, including one's fellow anglers.

It seems we live in a time when traditions are allowed to go by the boards rather easily. Some people think this is a good thing, for presumably it leaves us free to contemplate a future unfettered by the complications of the past—but it also necessarily calls for discarding the values and virtues of many good things that have gone before. Fly fishing, of course, is steeped in tradition, and the very breadth and depth of that tradition should hold it relatively safe from assault even in these unstructured times. But no tradition is completely safe unless it has disciples who are willing to preserve and extend it and keep it a living, growing thing.

What this means for a steelhead fly fisherman is that he should honor the contributions made by the pioneers of the sport even while he seeks to add to them through his own innovation and experiment. On a practical level this means continuing to tie and fish the fly patterns of Enos Bradner and Ralph Wahl and Walt Johnson and Wes Drain and Syd Glasso and George Keough and Mike Kennedy and dozens of others. It also means following the example of those who fought and won the first bureaucratic battles for the protection of steelhead and the establishment of the first fly-fishing-only and catch-and-release regulations, and this can only be done by pressing for more protection and more such regulations.

Above all it means continuing the struggle to rehabilitate streams like Deer Creek and the Coquihalla and to protect those rivers still free of the effects of man's depredations, and carrying on the fight to preserve and enhance wild steelhead runs wherever they are found. For implicit in accepting the pleasure of steelhead fly fishing is the obligation to do everything possible to preserve and protect it.

In addition to working for conservation, today's anglers must sustain the tradition by contributing their own new fly patterns and fishing methods, their own new books and works of art, their own new thoughts and theories, so that their generation will be well represented in the legends, lore, and literature of steelhead fly fishing. And I have no doubt that they will.

Respect for tradition comes easily and naturally to most fly fishermen, but respect for their fellow anglers may be a more difficult thing. There are more fishermen on today's rivers than ever before, and some are there for the wrong reasons or with no clear idea of why they are there at all. Partly this is because fly fishing has become an "in" sport and a big business, with social and commercial opportunities for all—or so it seems. Publications ranging from *Playboy* to *The Wall Street Journal* have declared fly fishing the essential sport for status-conscious trendy modern men, replacing golf as the most socially acceptable form of recreation.

*The Wall Street Journal* even went so far as to say that fly fishing savvy is practically required of anyone aspiring to be a corporate chief executive officer, which might not be a bad thing if it meant that the CEOs of forest products, mining, utility, and chemical industries would spend a little time on the rivers and get a close-up look at the real impacts some of their corporate activities have on steelhead fisheries.

One result of all this publicity and fanfare is the increasingly common spectacle of fishermen who have been quickly and superficially educated in fly-fishing "schools" and outfitted in the most stylish and expensive angling togs available from the mail-order catalogues and who then go out on the rivers merely for the purpose of being seen. Most have no concept of fly-fishing tradition or of the rules of etiquette that have long bound steelhead fly fishermen to a form of behavior that allows them to share the water, so instead they mostly just get in the way and make matters difficult for everyone else. It is hard to like and respect such "fishermen."

Yet in their own way these people do make a contribution to the sport, if only through the money they spend on it—at least some of which must find its way to state or federal wildlife funds where it is used to sustain and protect fisheries. And some do find fly fishing something more than just a means of attaining social status or business success; they discover it for the wonderful and intriguing sport it is, become interested in it and begin to explore it on all its many absorbing levels, just as all the rest of us have done. These fishermen are the ones we should grow to like and respect and invite to memberships in our clubs and federations so they can add their support and abilities to the struggle for conservation and the preservation of the fly-fishing tradition.

Even those who never will understand fly fishing—those who are out on the rivers just to be seen—deserve at least a little of our time and attention, if only to acquaint them politely with the rules by which the rest of us live and fish. By so doing we may keep intact the precepts of angling etiquette that have served most anglers long and well on our steelhead rivers—although, sadly, even among veteran steelhead fly fishers there are always a few selfish "hole hogs" who ignore the rules.

Another unpleasant aspect of the recent growth of fly-fishing popularity is the appearance of more people who use the sport mainly for their own economic or personal gain. It's sad but true that some people are in fly fishing only for what they can get out of it—money or commercial success or free trips or some measure of personal recognition, or perhaps all of these things together. Most will tell you that they really love the sport, and perhaps they do—but you might hear the same sort of statement from a man selling his sister on the street. These so-called professional fly fishermen are irritants, like mosquitoes, that must be put up with. We always have had them and probably we always shall have them, so we should try to tolerate them as best we can and be happy when they accidentally do something to benefit the sport—as some do, although usually more from coincidence than altruism.

That leaves all the rest of us, the great majority who love fly fishing because we have found in it greater and more consistent pleasure and reward than almost anything else life has to offer, those of us who have been fly fishing since long before it became a socially popular or commercially advantageous thing to do, plus those who may have taken up the sport for the wrong reasons but found the right ones. We owe it to ourselves to treat one another with appreciation and respect and extend the same courtesies we would always wish for ourselves.

Which brings us, finally, to the fish. Of all things deserving our appreciation and respect, the steelhead ranks foremost. Each returning fish is a small miracle, a survivor against the longest odds, an embodiment of courage and endurance almost beyond human understanding, a priceless gift from nature. The steelhead is what makes our sport possible; it is the source of all the tales told around campfires, the object of all the long days we spend in and around rivers, the final judge of all the artistry we put into our flies and all the skills we can bring to bear in our angling efforts. Without the steelhead we have nothing.

Such a prize deserves better treatment than it often receives. A steelhead is far too valuable to be caught only once. A steelhead that is caught and killed becomes not a trophy but a lump of cold flesh, and in death all its noble qualities are forever extinguished from the future of the runs. A fish that has survived all that a steelhead must survive deserves nothing more than to live and perpetuate the qualities that enabled it to survive. No angler should ever feel deprived for returning a fish to the river, for the memory of a good steelhead taken on the fly is just as vivid and precious if the fish is released as it would be if the fish were killed—in fact, the memory of a fish returned alive and well is somehow more satisfying, more complete, than if the fish's life had been abruptly terminated in the angler's hands.

So patience, skill, knowledge, appreciation and respect—all these are essential qualities for a good steelheader. But respect is the greatest of these—respect for the fish, for its life, for fellow anglers, for all things that give and sustain the life of rivers and the tradition of our sport.

# Epilogue

I HAVE always been glad that the colonists who settled this country landed first on the East Coast and worked their way slowly westward. Had it been the other way around I might now be living in a city the size of New York instead of Seattle, writing about steelhead fly fishing in the past tense instead of the present.

All that is purely a matter of luck, and try as he might to improve his skill so that he does not have to rely on luck, a steelhead fly fisherman never finds himself entirely free of the whims of fortune. For example, he must have the good luck to be born at the right place and the right time to grow up knowing a river at its best, or near best. I have always been grateful I had the good fortune to be born in the Pacific Northwest, right in the heart of steelhead country, in an environment and atmosphere that allowed me to grow up and become a fisherman. It's true, I suppose, that I was born too late to enjoy many rivers at their best, but I have had the pleasure of knowing some that were not far from that.

But if it is true that the members of my angling generation may not always have had the very best of things, I think in the future it will be clear that neither did we have the worst. Today's rivers may not have anywhere near as many fish as they had just a few years ago, but future rivers may have even less than we do now. The reasons are obvious and I have already touched on most of them—the cumulative destructive effects of logging, dams, pollution, development, and commercial fishing, especially high-seas drift-net fishing and unregulated Indian gill-net fisheries. The latter may be firmly grounded both in fairness and in legal fact, but they must also be carried out with some measure of responsibility, which so far has been lacking.

Yet not all fisheries problems are beyond the realm of our own responsibility. We who fish for sport must also put our own house in order, regulate our own habits, and minimize our own harvest if we expect to have anything left for the future.

All these matters, serious as they may be, pale to insignificance before such potential threats as global warming. If, as some predict, the so-called greenhouse effect from worldwide industrial air pollution will cause the atmosphere to warm, the polar caps to melt, the seas to rise, and the climate to change, then the catastrophic effects on steelhead runs—as well as nearly everything else—can scarcely be imagined.

With all this to consider, it is difficult to be optimistic about the future of steelhead or steelhead fishing. Yet one *must* be optimistic—for there is no other choice. We can only have hope that our own efforts and those of other fishermen to come, along with all those who care for the earth and seek to preserve it, will yet succeed in saving the steelhead and the rivers and the oceans and the air, or at least enough of all of them that future genera-

tions will have a healthy planet and an opportunity to share at least some of the pleasures we have enjoyed. So we must have hope for the future, plus the dedication to make that hope a reality; there is no other alternative.

I have already said that I envy those who are just starting out to fish for steelhead, and I still feel that way even in the face of impending environmental crisis—for they still have ahead of them all the great joys of fly-fishing discovery, along with the vigor and vision and enthusiasm of youth. They also will inherit an angling tradition that I think has been greatly enriched in the past few decades. Their angling lives will benefit not only from the innovations and knowledge gained during that time, but will be immeasurably enhanced by the literary and artistic contributions of men like Roderick Haig-Brown, Ralph Wahl, Tommy Brayshaw, Enos Bradner, and others of their time.

Even if their rivers may hold fewer fish than the streams of the present or the past, the steelhead fly fishermen of the future will also surely profit from the bright promise of new angling methods and technology. The technological revolution of the past couple of decades is bound to continue at an accelerating rate and certainly will produce new materials for rods and lines and leaders and flies and new tactics to employ them. I would like to be able to share in the excitement of trying all these new things.

I believe the future also necessarily will bring a new angling ethic, a new attitude of consideration toward fish and fishing that will be shared by anglers and the general public alike—part of a greater awareness and respect for rivers and the life in them and all the infinite interlocking threads of the environment that give and sustain life, not only in rivers but everywhere on the planet. I would like to live in a time when people will feel more kindly disposed toward these things—and, I hope, toward one another.

So I firmly hope, and strongly believe, that a hundred years from now, and for many more years beyond that, there will continue to be cold rivers that will plunge swiftly from snowcapped mountains to mingle with a clean, bright sea; that young life will still stir in the gravel of those rivers and strong fish will still head back to them; that fly fishermen will yet be there waiting to test their skill and tactics against these bold returning fish; and that those fishermen—though their tackle and methods may be beyond our guessing now—will still sense and feel and think as we do, indeed as all fishermen have done for as far back in human time as fishing goes.

To them we entrust the keeping of the rivers and the fish and the steelhead tradition. I am confident they will be in good hands.